Roll Back The Stone

Celebrating The Mystery
Of Lent And Easter
Through Drama

Kenneth Carlson
David H. Covington
John O. Eby
Kathy Martz
Will Rabert
Frank Ramirez
Carol Secord

CSS Publishing Company, Inc., Lima, Ohio

ROLL BACK THE STONE

For more information about CSS Publishing Company resources, visit our website at www.csspub.com or e-mail us at custserv@csspub.com or call (800) 241-4056.

Cover design by Chris Patton
ISBN 0-7880-2354-3

Table Of Contents

A Travesty Of Justice:
In The Shadow Of The Cross

Six Lenten Meditations

The Thorn
The Robe
The Nail
The Spear
The Shroud
The Stone

Kathy Martz

Lent is a time for re-examining baptismal vows and reflecting upon the cost of discipleship. It is a season of fasting and meditating in preparation for Easter; a time of recommitment for Christians all over the world. The following meditations are offered for spiritual contemplation during this Lenten season.

Series based on "Silent Witnesses" homily written by D. Scott Hewes. Used with permission.

Lenten prayers from the *Lutheran Book Of Worship*.

Hear ye! Hear ye!

Jesus of Nazareth was brought before Pilate and sentenced to death by crucifixion. A mockery of justice? You be the judge. Examine accounts from a cast of eyewitnesses telling about the victim, the charges, the trial, the verdict, and the sentence. Hear from the despised Thorn, the rumpled Robe, the hard Nail, the military Spear, the burial Shroud, and the huge Stone. Learn of their extraordinary encounters with this Jesus of Nazareth.

Ash Wednesday Meditation #1

Then Pilate took Jesus and scourged him. And the soldiers plaited a crown of thorns, and put it on his head, and arrayed him in a purple robe; they came up to him, saying "Hail, King of the Jews!" and struck him with their hands.

— John 19:1-3

The first witness to testify on behalf of this Jesus of Nazareth was a despised Thorn, crudely woven into a crown like a headpiece fit for a king.

The Thorn

As you have undoubtedly heard, I'm not very well liked and often considered to be a real "pain." I'm bare, pointed, grow every which way, and have been known to have a mind of my own. I'm not what you would call desirable. In fact, I am often considered to be worthless. But my life took a strange "twist" the day Jesus was brought before Pilate.

I was hanging out with my fellow thorns on the vine, enjoying the gentle breezes, minding my own business. I didn't have much to do with the others because, after all, our purpose was to deter others from getting too close. Isolation and dislike was just an expected response to our being. For us to cooperate, or even be concerned about one another, was unheard of. However, this relationship came into question when I noticed some soldiers coming across the field toward us. As they came closer, they drew their swords. "Oh, no," I thought, "This is it!"

I found myself concerned for our safety. I was right. The soldiers indiscriminately hacked, chopped, and cut down many of the vines. I was surprised they didn't just set fire to us right then and there. But, instead, we were collected and transported to their barracks. Our total destruction was not their primary concern. They obviously had something else in mind.

In the barracks, strange things began to happen. I remember feeling dizzy as the vine I was on was twisted and turned over and over. It was rather peculiar that we were working together, almost cooperating with each other! Although a bit unorganized, together we managed to form a rather crude circle. With the guidance of a soldier, we were fashioned into a primitive crown. I couldn't help but wonder why anyone would go to so much trouble and pain.

But the main focus in the room was not completely on our transformation into something useful, but rather on some upcoming event. The mood seemed political in nature, but not without emotional outbursts. Some felt that a crucifixion was called for while others saw no criminal intent whatsoever. The consensus seemed to be that even though he was innocent, he needed to be taken care of once and for all. Perplexing, indeed.

While I was contemplating our future, we were whisked away and taken out into an adjacent courtyard. There stood an impressive edifice, obviously a governmental structure of some sort, demanding homage and respect from those who gathered in its presence. The atmosphere was strangely tense, as if waiting for some unknown event of great importance. There we were assembled among the masses — crude, rough, despised thorns. Imagine!

Curious, I stretched as far as I could to get a closer look at what was about to happen. It was hard for me to see, since I had ended up on the bottom pointing down. I was able to catch a glimpse of a large crowd milling around in the courtyard. I could only speculate as to the anticipated event — a coronation of a king or governor or prince. But what role could we possibly play?

9

Suddenly, a hush came over the crowd and all eyes were on us as we were paraded to the center of the courtyard. Snickers and jeers could be heard as if we were about to be part of something despicable. But, I couldn't see anyone who looked like the recipient of such a gesture. In fact, the only one who caught my attention was an itinerant preacher who was on trial for blasphemy. Then I recalled the soldiers' discussion about their intent to persecute an innocent man.

As we made our way through the angry crowd over to this preacher, a strange thing began to happen. The closer we got, the more alive and stronger we became. Just the opposite should have been happening. After all, we had been severed from our lifeline in the field and were expecting to become weak, shrivel, and die. But then, there was nothing usual or predictable about that day.

Two soldiers carefully lifted us high above the crowd for all to see. Meanwhile, others put a rumpled rag of a robe around the accuser's shoulders. The crowd paid him homage by laughing, jeering, and even spitting. Suddenly, we were hoisted in the direction of the man's head, oblivious to the fact that we would certainly inflict pain.

There was nothing we could do! We were entwined so tightly together movement was impossible. We cringed as we were lifted past his face, and were able to catch a glimpse of his eyes. They cried out for compassion. Although deeply touched, there was little we could do. We simply had no control over the situation. Despite our combined objections, we were brutally shoved onto his head. We were pushed with a sense of hatred and ridicule, driving the crown deeper and deeper into his skull.

In that split instant, when we were forced into his forehead, we went through more emotions than any thorn could possibly imagine. How could they do this? How could they be so cruel to one another? How could they be so cruel to someone who showed only love in his eyes? How dare they use us in this inhuman way, to inflict pain on an innocent man and cause him to suffer?

Initially we felt horror and disgust toward those who had used us in such an inhumane way. But then we went through a change of feelings; a change in character and being. The instant we came in contact with his flesh, a feeling shot through us that was beyond anything we had ever felt before. There was a sense of life and living that surpassed even being attached to our roots in the field. It was a different and more powerful life flowing around us. It caused us to feel warm and peaceful. It was something that flowed from him to us. We were inflicting pain and he gave warmth, love, and peace in return. How illogical!

He returned love for pain. He gave warmth in a blizzard of hatred. He poured out his blood of suffering and warmed worthless thorns like us. What kind of man was this? He was not like other men. How blessed we were to touch the flesh of such a special person! Now I know why we were separated from our former roots. He transformed our feelings of worthlessness into beings of immeasurable value.

How I envy you humans! Oh, don't get me wrong; I'm thankful and content with my role ... but oh, how blessed you are! I know now that the same blood that spilled onto me was shed for you. How blessed you are that you are invited to live with him ... forever! Imagine, an eternity to experience what I had for just a few moments! You see, he did all of that for you!

Ash Wednesday Prayer

Almighty and ever-living God, you hate nothing you have made and you forgive the sins of all who are penitent. Create in us new and honest hearts, so that, truly repenting of our sins, we may obtain from you, the God of all mercy, full pardon and forgiveness; through your Son, Jesus Christ our Lord, who lives and reigns with you and the Holy Spirit, one God, now and forever. Amen.

Lenten Meditation #2

Then the soldiers of the governor took Jesus into the praetorian, and they gathered the whole battalion before him. And they stripped him and put a scarlet robe upon him, and plaiting a crown of thorns they put it on his head, and put a reed in his right hand. — Matthew 27:27-29

After hearing of how a despised Thorn was crudely woven into a crown fit for the king, it seems highly unlikely that a proud, conceited Robe could offer further insight into the plight of this Jesus of Nazareth. But, then stranger things have happened.

The Robe

As you can see, I'm not a run-of-the-mill piece of fabric for the commoner. I am made of the finest quality material ever woven into cloth. The greatest care was taken when I was made. I was flawless; acceptable even to royalty. I was cared for and given the finest texture, the softest sheen, and the smoothness of delicate skin. After that, I was soaked in a solution that gave me the deepest of royal, scarlet color. I then was handed over to the best tailors, and artistically patterned into a royal robe fit for a king. I was discovered immediately to be the finest garment available in the province.

I was picked from scores of others to serve a most noble ruler, and given a position of honor in the governor's royal closet. Thus, it's no wonder, I was privy to the exclusive functions only royalty attended. I made grand appearances at parties, banquets, and affairs of state. Soon I became the governor's most prized garment. Robes of lesser quality were rejected, but that is the privilege of being the best.

As I look back, I fear my ego may have gotten the best of me, as I slightly overestimated my importance. For one day, a finer robe was brought to the palace; a robe that was imported from some exotic country, fresh and new. A robe that was free of any signs of experience, with no stains or weak spots. I was, needless to say, devastated. To add injury to insult, I was hung in the closet next to the other unused, neglected clothing. Later, I was to end up in a pile with other discarded, abandone garments — a mere rag!

As I became more and more wrinkled from being shoved about the pile, I began to observe some stains on me that I had never noticed before. I began to realize how much in common I had with the other rags in the pile. I was stained and worn. The very stains I used to deny, now seemed to taunt me.

I found myself making friends with the other clothes in the pile, often gossiping to pass the time. One afternoon, we were distracted by a loud commotion outside the window. We could hear an angry crowd in the courtyard yelling, "Crucify him!"

The governor could find no reason to execute the man, but the crowd became indignant, and the governor gave into the pressure. Nervously, we huddled together, finding security in the mass of worthless and forgotten material. The crowd's demeanor went from an unexpected, but welcomed silence, to a full-fledged uproar. As the intensity of the crowd increased, we sensed our security being threatened.

A soldier came in and began rummaging through the pile. I felt his hand tighten around my hem. I was pulled and tugged until finally freed from the middle of the pile. I was a mess! I was wrinkled, soiled, and torn. But the soldier was smiling as though he had found the prize he had been looking for. He began to laugh out loud as he wadded me up and headed for the courtyard.

As we made our way through the crowd, I was flaunted about for all to see. It was most embarrassing, I was humiliated! It certainly wasn't my fault that I was wrinkled and stained. Why was I being made a fool?

Suddenly, I caught a glimpse of the one on trial. He was standing in the center of the courtyard facing the throne. His head was down as if he was completely devastated. I noticed that he wore simple sandals, a common garment, and the most hideous head covering I had ever seen: He was wearing a crudely woven crown — made of thorns! His hands were bound. His forehead stained with the blood that flowed from the puncture wounds caused by the thorns. He was still ... both in body and voice.

In contrast to his stillness, the crowd yelled, "Crucify him!" And then someone would walk by mocking him.

As the tempo of the crowd picked up, I was brought out to the center of the courtyard for all to see. I was humiliated beyond my wildest dreams, degraded in front of the governor and all those people. Once the pride of the governor, I had been reduced to a used, rumpled, rag; my pride nonexistent. I was feeling sorry for myself, and desperately wanted to retreat to the security of the once despised pile of rags, but this self-indulgent pity lasted only a short time.

Somehow, I had been chosen to play a part in this mockery, to give the appearance of a royalty, stained, wrinkled, and worn. Draped around the accused's shoulders, I found myself distracted. He became the focus of my attention. He was more than a governor. He was a king, the pride of his Father, and was being degraded in front of all his subjects.

Strange things began to happen to me: the wrinkles on my outside disappeared on the inside. The worn spots showed on the outside, but on the inside the weave of the fabric was as perfect as the day I had been set free from the loom.

And the stains, let me tell you about the stains. I had managed to collect a lifetime's worth of stains. I was covered with every imaginable dirt, grit, and grime. Oh, I had fooled myself into ignoring them for years, but all the while they were there. The irony is that even though the wrinkles and the worn parts seemed better — as if healed — the stains were intensified and became clearer when I was on the shoulders of this Jesus of Nazareth.

As I hung there on his shoulders, several drops of his blood fell on me and splattered everywhere. The blood touched parts of me that were stained from a lifetime of abuse and neglect. Amazingly, the stains disappeared as though they had never existed. My color returned to a brilliance far beyond that of my original, royal splendor. Each time a drop of blood reached a blemish in my being, I could feel the transforming power that removed every hint of stain. Oh, what a marvelous feeling! What a marvelous reality!

Here, look at me. Do you see any stains? Do you? Oh, sure, I'm, still wrinkled and worn in places; that's because I'm old and getting older. But there are no stains on me at all! The blood of that humble man who was crucified, has washed me beyond "clean"; his blood has washed me pure!

Yes, I am cleansed with his blood, and so are you! That is what this whole incident is about. You see, I was once again cast aside after the soldiers had made their point, and mocked the one called Jesus. But, his blood was shed to make pure all people — people like you who have been stained with all manner of grime. His blood was shed to cleanse all people for all time who accept his cleansing by faith. Of course, there will be more stains as time goes on, but, all you need to do is ask this one who was mocked and crucified that day to wash them away with his blood. He will, you know!

And that's not all: after he has cleansed you, you needn't worry about being cast into the corner "rag pile" of life, for the people whom he cleanses, he takes with him to live as royalty in the palace of his Father. You have been washed with the blood of the King of kings!

Lenten Prayer

Lord God, our strength, the battle of good and evil rages within and around us, and our ancient foe tempts us with his deceits and empty promises. Keep us steadfast in your word and when we fall, raise us again and restore us through your Son, Jesus Christ our Lord, who lives and reigns with you and the Holy Spirit, one God, now and forever. Amen.

Lenten Meditation #3

So they took Jesus, and he went out bearing his own cross, to the place called the place of a skull, which is called in Hebrew Golgotha. There they crucified him, with two others, one on either side, and Jesus between them. Pilate also wrote a title and put it on the cross; it read, "Jesus of Nazareth, the King of the Jews." Many of the Jews read this title, for the place where Jesus was crucified was near the city; and was written in Hebrew, in Latin, and in Greek. The chief priests of the Jews then said to Pilate, "Do not write, 'The King of the Jews,' but, 'This man said, I am King of the Jews.'" Pilate answered, "What I have written I have written."

— John 19:17-22

The Robe's touching account of the injustice heaped upon Jesus of Nazareth and the healing that radiated from within is hard to comprehend. It suggests the absurdity of the situation — a mere mockery of a trial. The more we learn about the crucifixion of Jesus, the more confused we become. The Nail that touched the hand of Jesus that fateful day has yet another puzzling account to offer.

The Nail

I may look like just a nail to you, but I didn't start out that way. My beginning is almost as old as time itself and involved basic human ingenuity: mining, smelting, molding, and shaping. I began as a pile of dust pressed into a rock, held together by a common bond. I was heated, melted, and poured into a mold, thus acquiring my familiar shape. Finally, I was stored in a container with others of my kind to wait until someone had need of me.

On the surface, I give the appearance of being cold and hard. To some, my existence may even appear boring. I suppose, in a way it is. I spent a lifetime waiting to be chosen simply by random, to perform some menial task. Even then, my uneventful existence would continue until I rusted or retired for future assignments. It's not easy to admit that my usefulness was often activated by a well-meaning hit on the head from a hammer.

But I, too, had ambitions! I had hoped to be an important part in the construction of a fine building, or palace, or at least a monument of some sort. Why, even a cow stall would be preferable to stagnating with my peers.

My existence was to change in a way never expected. For me, one day was much like another. It consisted of endless hours of contemplating my seemingly uneventful future in a bin surrounded by others with a similar fate. My boredom was suddenly interrupted when a take-charge officer of the crown literally marched into the establishment. His presence was instantly noticed by all. He pushed his way through the meandering mass of casual on-lookers to the bin where I resided. I was struck by his determination and sense of mission. With mechanical precision, he randomly grabbed three of us from the pile, bagged and weighed us. After completing his purchase, he proceeded to make his exit as memorable as his entrance.

Even though I was "chosen" purely by chance, my hopes were high that this was going to be an important assignment. After all, a government official had need of my services. But, alas, my ambitions were quickly shattered.

As soon as my head was out of the sack, I could see that a horrible event was about to take place. Mass confusion was before me. As I tried to comprehend what was happening, it became hauntingly clear. The process leading up to a crucifixion was well under way — the death march had begun. I was sure that since the condemned man was already carrying his own cross up the hill, my job was *not* to hold the cross together. So why was I chosen, and for what purpose?

Later to my utter disgust, I learned that I had been chosen to secure the accused to the cross. I took little comfort in the fact that two fellow nails were to assist. There was little to do, but watch and wait.

A parade-like stream formed as the death march proceeded up the hill where the crucifixion was to take place. The participants sent mixed messages. Hecklers were cheering and applauding as the soldiers prodded the condemned man along. Their cry, "Crucify him!" sounded much like a cheer for victory at the arena.

Others quietly prayed and pleaded for mercy, "But he's guilty of no crime! He's innocent! You can't kill an innocent man!"

This diversion of opinion was very unsettling; what if he really were innocent? I'd be helping an injustice to take place! I was a victim of circumstance. I had no choice. These thoughts were abruptly interrupted when I found myself heading toward the cross lying on the ground.

I could see a man on the cross, arms outstretched, eyes looking up into the sky. He didn't look like a criminal.... Suddenly, I was shoved against the flesh of his hand. It all happened so quickly; I barely had time to comprehend the significance of what was about to take place. At the time, I thought it odd that his hand was wide open, as if inviting me to secure it to the cross. It wasn't clenched in anger, as I thought it should, but rather opened and relaxed.

As I touched his hand, I felt a strange sense of power — a power that could have resisted any intruding force. There was a strength beyond description, a strength that should have caused me to bend in submission, but didn't. In addition to the strength, there was a softness — not a weakness, but an all encompassing feeling of calm, peace, and tranquility. There was a warmth there too, almost an invitation to touch him, and even to be driven through his hand into the rough wood of the cross.

I braced myself for penetrating the bone and flesh of the outstretched hand. But, to my amazement, I passed right through to the rugged cross beneath without even breaking a bone! This was no ordinary common criminal.

As the cross was tediously lifted into place, the two other nails assisting me didn't seem to lessen the sudden and overpowering strain. At first we felt a sense of crushing weight. But, then the load seemed to lessen, as if we weren't alone. The weight shifted onto the weary shoulders of the accused.

As we struggled with the physical weight, this Jesus of Nazareth struggled, too. He wrestled with something other than just human poundage. He faced the emotional strain of sorrow and despair. My physical burden was lessened as one of my peers came to rescue, helping to support the limp body. But, this Jesus seemed to have a strength that went beyond the immediate pain of the flesh. He began to minister to the anguish and despair of the crowd of accusers. He cried out for their forgiveness!

He died rather quickly, after only three hours. His death seemed more than just the end to the undeserved torture he suffered on that cross. It was as if he had almost chosen to die, as if he was really in control, even as his life ebbed.

15

The soldiers returned to make sure that the death had indeed occurred, and then relieved us of our duties. We were tossed aside; left to contemplate the extraordinary events we had just witnessed.

Those powerful events drew us together and gave us a sense of being. We no longer were just simple, hollow shells without purpose, but were bonded together with an inner sense of contentment. This humble Jesus had conveyed an overwhelming sense of strength and power.

Even though weather and time take its toll on us, we won't mind. For you see, our highest ambitions were fulfilled that day. Your highest ambitions can also be fulfilled. You have the promise of eternal life from this humble man who was crucified on the cross that day; life with him in a place where there are no crucifixions, no inhumane acts of hatred or injustice, but a place filled with love and power. How blessed you are with his promise of eternal life!

Lenten Prayer

Eternal Lord, your kingdom has broken into our troubled world through the life, death, and resurrection of your Son. Help us to hear your Word and obey it, so that we become instruments of your redeeming love through your Son, Jesus Christ our Lord, who lives and reigns with you and the Holy Spirit, one God, now and forever. Amen.

Lenten Meditation #4

Since it was the day of Preparation, in order to prevent the bodies from remaining on the cross on the Sabbath (for that Sabbath was a high day), the Jews asked Pilate that their legs might be broken, and they might be taken away. So the soldiers came and broke the legs of the first, and of the other who had been crucified with him; but when they came to Jesus and saw that he was already dead, they did not break his legs. But one of the soldiers pierced his side with a spear, and at once there came out blood and water. He who saw it has borne witness — his testimony is true, and he knows that he tells the truth — that you also may believe. For these things took place that the scripture might be fulfilled, "Not a bone of his shall be broken." And again another scripture says, "They shall look on him whom they have pierced." — John 19:31-37

The Nail's account of what happened the day Jesus was crucified left us pondering. Perhaps an "official" point of view would be helpful. Hear how the shadow of the cross brought relief to a proud, military Spear left out in the scorching, afternoon sun.

The Spear

I am an official weapon of the government, with a position of great responsibility and authority. I have fought fierce battles against enemies of superior numbers and force. I have seen men die fighting for the honor of their country and king. I have pierced the flesh of anarchists, terrorists, and criminals without missing a beat. I have served courageous soldiers and kings as well as yellow-bellied cowards. I am a loyal and conscientious subject of the crown.

I have never been broken; always flawlessly polished and sharpened. My handle, rubbed with the finest oils, has never shown nicks or cracks from the pressures of battle. With the proper care and respect, I have managed to outlast lesser weapons.

I am here now because what I have witnessed needs to be told, and told accurately. As I look back, the whole series of events was confusing: the charges, the trial, the verdict, the sentence, and the victim.

When I first encountered the victim, he was on trial for heresy and treason. He was considered a threat to the government, because he allegedly referred to himself as "king." I didn't see him as much of a threat to anyone; his followers weren't even armed!

Personally, I could find no real crime that he had committed. Trumped up charges were based on hearsay. Witnesses were constantly changing their stories and contradicting themselves. Even the judges were unsure and passed the case from one to another, not wanting to make the final decision.

The matter was finally turned over to the governor. Originally, he pronounced the victim innocent. But unfortunately, an incensed, angry mob frightened and intimidated him. An innocent man was sentenced to death by crucifixion. He was to be crucified along with two other recently convicted criminals. Imagine a kind and decent man associated with such an element. I have never seen such a mockery of justice!

After the bogus sentence was finally handed down, an unconventional crowd gathered for the traditional death march. Ironically, my past performance in such situations made me the perfect candidate for the assignment. I was thrust into a bizarre situation over which I had no control. My blade polished and sharpened, I prepared for the worst.

As the march proceeded, it was obvious that the condemned man was in no shape to carry his own cross. He appeared weak from the recent beatings, and was bloody about the face from the crown of thorns placed on his head. Several times he began to stumble from the weight of the cross. I was used to prod him along, rapping him sharply on the back of the legs.

The journey up the hill was not uneventful. The crowd was totally unpredictable. Some were very emotional as they pleaded for his innocence, while others spit and cursed as we passed by. Some even applauded when I prodded him along. The whole thing was quite confusing!

No wonder this was one of the strangest assignments I could remember. Normally, I enjoyed my work and faced each assignment with the proper enthusiasm required. But this day was different. I performed my duty, but without my usual enthusiasm and conviction. All of my experience and superior training could not prevent a nagging feeling of betrayal. Instead of anticipating a victorious ending, I found myself hoping for a humane ending to this madness.

When we reached the top of the hill, I assumed that I would be at attention during the rest of the proceedings, and thus not have to participate. Even though my nature was to be part of the action, I found myself pleased to be thrust into the middle of an argument between a couple of guards, quite removed from the ongoing proceedings. It seemed a disagreement had erupted over who would get to keep the condemned man's robe. (As was the custom, the clothing of the condemned was one of the perks of crucifixion duty.) The whole argument seemed rather ridiculous to me, as the cloak was a simple, torn, and wrinkled garment hardly worth fighting over. But this served as a diversion to my moral dilemma.

It was, unfortunately, only temporary; I was soon tossed aside for a pair of dice. My intimidating nature was not required, as the soldiers decided to let a roll of the dice settle their dispute. In their haste to reach a settlement, I found myself lying in the dirt beneath the cross, waiting for the victor to claim his spoils.

As I lie there, I began to beat myself up for being such a coward and letting this man's injustice affect me. If that wasn't bad enough, I felt the sun's intensity attacking my whole being — drying out my delicate handle, and setting my sharp blade aglow.

Miraculously, the sun shifted, and soon I lay in the shadow of the cross. I began to feel relief from the heat of the day. I was thankful that he was there to give relief. It was truly amazing how different I felt in the shadow of that cross; the cross distracted my attention, as well as my humiliation.

Glancing upward, I couldn't help but notice the cross looming above me. My view from the ground provided me with a rather unique, unobstructed view of the humble man hanging on the cross. With his head hung down, I could plainly see the agonizing expression on his face. It revealed a hurt beyond the physical pain inflicted by the beatings, the puncture wounds, and the penetrating nails. His whole being silently cried out in agony. His eyes reflected the painful betrayal of his own kind. Even though I could clearly read the anguish on his face, his words were those of love and compassion.

It was difficult for me to comprehend how a man so mistreated could find the strength and love to ask for the forgiveness of his accusers. With love and conviction, he cried out for their salvation, "Father, forgive them, for they know not what they do!"

With these the words of forgiveness, the agony on his face turned to a look of assurance as though he knew that his final request had been granted. Only then did he look at peace.

I was distracted from the emotional drama taking place and abruptly snatched from the serenity of the shadow of the cross. Unaware of the events to follow, I was drafted back into action. I was carefully polished, sharpened, and prepared for duty. Actually, I was quite relieved for the opportunity to return to my role as protector and defender of the crown, and found myself desperately searching for the required commitment and determination.

Activity at the crucifixion was winding down, as the main crowd had long since dispersed. A few stragglers, praying and lamenting, were interspersed with the small number of remaining soldiers. The soldiers were there to attend to the bodies — they had to be removed from the crosses as per the religious custom of the day. To speed up the dying process, the soldiers were ordered to break the criminals' legs.

They went about their assignment with a sense of methodical precision. The two criminals hanging on either side of the one called "king" were taken care of first without incident. When the soldiers approached the "king," they were unable to detect any life in his body. Not wishing to break his legs unnecessarily, they turned to me to help confirm their suspicions.

His gaze was gone; his eyes closed in death. Even though his heart had stopped, it seemed as though his forgiveness was still there. But the soldiers had a job to complete, and so I was called upon to pierce the side of this humiliated man as a final act in a day of unthinkable atrocities. What I found there was totally unexpected: a broken heart, a heart, which had beaten for love and forgiveness had been broken by hate and rejection.

As I was pulled from the lifeless body, blood and water flowed out. Immediately, the blood that had touched me affected me: I felt sharper and shinier than ever before. A sense of newness surrounded me as if I had been cleansed from my sins. As the water engulfed me, I knew that he had forgiven me for my role in the events of that day.

We can all share the assurance that the blood and water flowed forth with the power to cleanse, to purify, to restore, and to renew! Isn't it curious how a painful wound was used by God to allow his love and forgiveness to flow out for all the world?

Lenten Prayer

God of all mercy, by your power to heal and to forgive, graciously cleanse us from all sin and make us strong through your Son, Jesus Christ our Lord, who lives and reigns with you and the Holy Spirit, one God, now and forever. Amen.

Lenten Meditation #5

And when evening had come, since it was the day of Preparation, that is, the day before the Sabbath, Joseph of Arimathea, a respected member of the council, who was also himself looking for the kingdom of God, took courage and went to Pilate, and asked for the body of Jesus. And Pilate wondered if he were already dead; and summoning the centurion, he asked him whether he was already dead. And when he learned from the centurion that he was dead, he granted the body to Joseph. And he brought a linen shroud, and taking him down, wrapped him in the linen shroud, and laid him in a tomb which had been hewn out of the rock;

— Mark 15:42-46a

The official account of the Spear gave credence to the testimony of the others, the Thorn, the Robe, and the Nail, who were eyewitnesses to the crucifixion of the one called Jesus. One of the last to touch this extraordinary man was the Shroud, who honored the Jewish burial custom of wrapping the body. Although the Shroud was not a witness to the actual events leading up to and including the crucifixion, the account is quite compelling and deserves our attention.

The Shroud

I come from a very humble beginning. I started out as a flaxseed, and developed into a plant with beautiful blue flowers. A simple weed in the field, I was selected for a very special purpose. I was chosen to be woven into fine linen.

The transformation from flax to linen is rather complicated, and requires unselfish corporation. There is a spinning and weaving that takes place. Plants become threads; threads become linen. It may surprise you to know that the texture of fine linen is often as smooth as silk. It offers a beautiful shine with amazing strength.

Like many others, I had high expectations, and envisioned myself a fabric of majestic quality. Skilled spinners and weavers had worked their magic to create just such an exquisite piece of linen; linen fine enough to adorn palaces. So it was easy to imagine myself a stately fabric surrounded by royalty. But, apparently, it was not to be.

I found myself in a small, out of the way shop, waiting to be sold. My high quality was almost unnoticed in the maze of sameness. The order of my importance was determined simply by my position in the pile. Waiting my turn was pure torture. Who would buy me? Where would I go? What would I become?

Finally, I made it to the top of the pile. My head was filled with thoughts of grandeur; would I adorn a fine table, or be on display for all to appreciate my beautiful weave. As if an answer to my contemplation, a well-dressed man, Joseph of Arimathea, came into the shop to purchase a piece of linen. I could tell he was a man of importance, and only hoped to have a place of honor in his house.

But, once again it seemed my dream was to be denied. Joseph was in need of a cloth for a burial shroud. (It was the Jewish custom to wrap the body in linen strips layered with myrrh and aloes in preparation for burial.) I was chosen to be that piece of linen. Me, wrapped around a corpse, of all things! Buried away in a dark, damp tomb, never to be seen or appreciated again! I began to wish I had stayed in the field to die and go to seed. At least then I would have served a purpose and left my mark. But, to be stuck away in a hole....

As Joseph and I left for parts unknown, I began to contemplate my unthinkable plight, to cover a corpse. With thoughts of disgust running through my mind, I almost missed the conglomeration of spices piled on the side of the road. Interestingly enough, these were the very spices used in preparing a body for burial. Nicodemus was busily unloading the 100 pounds of myrrh and aloes needed for preparation.

Spread haphazardly about the ground, the aloes and myrrh appeared to be less enthusiastic about the prospect of spending their lifetime with a corpse than I was. Leaving us to our own devices, Joseph and Nicodemus left to go retrieve the body. Consoling one another in our misfortune, the future was looking pretty grim, indeed.

Lying around on the cold, damp ground, the aloes and myrrh and I quickly lost our inhibitions and began to comfort one another in our hour of need. Even though we had little in common, it was nice to know that we weren't alone. Together, we would make the best of an impossible situation.

Our fate was becoming a dismal reality. Not only were we to wrap a corpse, but we learned it was to be the corpse of a criminal who had been crucified! Why didn't they just toss him into the burning garbage pit behind the hill with the others who had been crucified? Criminals weren't entitled to a burial. Why was he so special?

As if to answer our burning questions, Joseph and Nicodemus returned with the body and gently laid it on ground. At first glance, it was just a body, limp and lifeless. Scars and fresh wounds could be seen about the head and hands, not unexpected for the corpse of a criminal. Upon closer observation, it became obvious this was not the body of a common criminal at all.

The body appeared to be peaceful and relaxed, is if in deep slumber. Strangely, the wounds and scars seemed to be fading, as if representing the undeserved pain and suffering. Kindness and innocence emanated from the cold ground where the body lay. The lifeless body lay in limbo, waiting.

Those involved with the preparation of the body arrived, anxious to complete their task prior to the Sabbath. Anointing the body with aloes and myrrh was an important part of the religious preparation for burial, allowing the loved ones to administer one final act of devotion.

Arranging the aloes and myrrh in proper sequence, the preparation of the body was gently attended to. Watching the aloes and myrrh adorn the body was a sight to behold. As they came in contact with the body, I could see an immediate change in their purity and vibrancy. It was unlike anything I had ever seen before. The love with which they were gently rubbed and massaged into the lifeless body filled the air. The site lost its dark, damp, hopelessness and began to take on an atmosphere of anticipation and renewal.

I was so taken with the events of preparation that I forgot to be disgusted and incensed with the prospect of being wrapped about a corpse! When I first touched the body of the crucified man, there was a sensation that passed through all of my strands and bridged the very gaps in my weave. It was as though I was being fused into one, solid mass; a mass with uncommon strength, the texture of the finest silk, and a softness to surpass the flesh of an infant. I experienced what the aloes and myrrh had felt when they came in contact with the body. This was not the body of a criminal at all, but someone with special powers and purpose.

There was no doubt that he was dead; vital functions had ceased. Yet, there was this strange sensation that made *me* feel alive and strong. There was a sense of confidence and security as I was allowed to hold his precious body resting in death.

My existence took on a new sense of importance. I knew that I had been set apart from the time I was a sprout in the field. I was not just one of the flax of the earth; I was a small part of a great plan to accomplish something magnificent. I didn't understand it, but I knew it.

Later, the body was taken to the grave, where he was laid to rest. The tomb was sealed tightly with a huge stone. Darkness, quiet, and emptiness surrounded us.

Resigned to the cold reality of our situation, the aloes, myrrh, and I vowed to approach our duties with care and sensitivity. We would adorn and protect this body from future harm. Thus, we carefully redesigned our space so as to comfortably enter eternity.

We lay motionless for a couple days. It wasn't so bad.... Then a slight movement disturbed our restful existence. The movement became more regular and increased in intensity. I tightened my grip as the aloes and myrrh were jostled about. The movement had become rhythmic as though his silenced heart was pumping once again, pumping life back into his limp body! It was the movement of life!

Then something beyond imagination occurred, something lacking logical explanation. As the movement intensified, we strained to maintain our position. The aloes and myrrh were huddled together, frantically clinging to my disjointed strips. One moment we were fighting to surround the body; the next moment the body was gone! I had been transformed into a shroud of life!

Oh, I didn't give life to the crucified one. But I was allowed to serve him by holding him only as long as he chose to be held. For you see, he was never really bound. And now, neither are you! He is free from that which held him, and so are you! I used to think death was the end. Obviously, it's only the beginning.

Lenten Prayer

Almighty God, you give us the joy of celebrating our Lord's resurrection. Give us also the joys of life in your service, and bring us at last to the full joy of life eternal; through your Son, Jesus Christ our Lord, who lives and reigns with you and the Holy Spirit, one God, now and forever. Amen.

Lenten Meditation #6

And Joseph took the body, and wrapped it in a clean linen shroud, and laid it in his own new tomb, which he had hewn in the rock; and he rolled a great stone to the door of the tomb, and departed. — Matthew 27:59-60

The Thorn, the Robe, the Nail, the Spear, and the Shroud all played significant parts in the final hours of this Jesus of Nazareth's life. Their accounts have been remarkable, to say the least. But the Stone's account of the strange circumstances that led to the "disappearance" of Jesus is quite amazing.

The Stone

I find it somewhat interesting that you would want to hear from me, since I have spent so much of life just resting in one place. My existence had been uneventful until the "disappearance" of that Jesus of Nazareth.

My metamorphosis took place over a long period of time. I witnessed a beautiful garden take shape around me. Its gentle beauty made my statue-like existence bearable. I was just another common garden-variety stone — huge, rough, heavy, strong, solid, nothing special or unusual. But then, what could I expect? I wasn't one of those flashy, valuable little gems destined to be fashioned into fine jewelry. It seemed my lot in life was just to be, and I was quite good at it. Solitude and I were good friends. Then, without warning, my solitude was interrupted.

It seemed a couple of men weren't quite as content with my appearance as I. They disapproved so violently with my facade that they began to tediously chip away at my rough exterior. It had taken centuries to achieve such a stature, so why these men suddenly felt compelled to remodel it was rather insulting. But the longer they worked, chipping and shaping, the more intrigued I became. I was becoming smoother, more uniform in shape, almost round-like. The transformation was quite amazing. My rough edges were gone. I was given a shape that apparently had a purpose; a purpose worth contemplating.

My new identity was quite perplexing, and so I began to speculate as to my usage. Was I to be a grinding wheel, or perhaps a base for a monument? My head was filled with thoughts of excitement about what lay ahead. I was rudely interrupted and tilted up on my rounded rim. I experienced a strange spinning sensation. When the sensation stopped, I discovered I had been rolled toward an opening in the side of a small hill.

I had often admired that particular hill from afar, and often wondered what it looked like up close. It turned out to be a tomb that belonged to Joseph, a rather rich and influential member of the church council. As I rolled slowly by the opening, I caught a quick glimpse inside. Just as expected, it was a rather dark and rather uninviting space, with a slab-like table inside.

I was left resting against the side of the hill, just past the opening. I noticed some smaller stones had been wedged underneath me to help secure my position. I couldn't help but wonder what was in store for me. The more I thought about it, the more I began to realize my purpose was to seal the tomb. Odd, why would someone go to the trouble of sealing a tomb?

My concentration was broken by a distant conversation. It seemed a crucifixion was to take place not far from the garden I overlooked. I didn't pay much attention because surely it wouldn't affect me. After all, the tomb I was guarding was for a man of greater importance, not a common criminal. Yet, the events of that day did affect me and everyone else as well.

I didn't have to wait very long. Things began to happen around noon. Suddenly, the whole world became very dark, as if something evil had swallowed up the sun. From the darkness emerged an overwhelming sense of impending destruction. The ground beneath me shook with a force I had never experienced. Vibrations and tremors could be felt everywhere; a full-fledged earthquake resulted. It was as if the heavens and earth were having a violent reaction to the events of the day — the unjustified crucifixion of the one called Jesus.

Three hours passed. The sky finally cleared and the earth became calm again. Looking over the aftermath, I found I had weathered the storm with minimal damage. I had held my ground, with a little help from the stones wedged beneath me. Lazily, I dozed off in the warm sunshine that had returned. But my rest was again disturbed by the sound of people walking in the garden.

Among those walking in the garden was Joseph, the owner of the tomb, and Nicodemus. They were carrying a body wrapped in a linen shroud. They entered the tomb and rested the body on the slab. I could only speculate it had to be one of criminals from the afternoon's activity. It seemed strange that the tomb was to be used for a criminal recently crucified. After all, it was for Joseph's personal use, and to relinquish it for a common criminal seemed rather ridiculous.

Curious as to why this particular criminal should be given such extraordinary treatment, I focused on the body. As expected, it was limp and lifeless. But strangely, it emitted a sense of power and strength. The shroud neatly held the spices and oils around the body, as if preparing it for some impending mission. The wounds on the body seemed intensified through the layers of myrrh and aloes. The care in burial preparation showed a love and concern far beyond what a common criminal deserved. But this was no ordinary body.

After placing the body in the tomb, Joseph and Nicodemus painfully wedged me into the opening. Satisfied that the tomb was sufficiently sealed, the two departed. Later, guards were stationed beside me to make sure that it remained sealed. The guards seemed quite unnecessary, as I was wedged rather snuggly into the opening, with little chance of coming loose. But they, too, had their orders, and proceeded to secure the parameter. I tried to rationalize the situation, and took comfort in the fact that I would certainly out last the guards.

But, I was once again disturbed as the guards painstakingly pushed me aside. They reluctantly escorted two of the women who had previously been with Joseph and Nicodemus into the tomb. They carefully watched as the women were allowed to complete their unfinished task of anointing the body for final resting. At least the guards seemed to have a purpose. As their final act, they called upon me to secure the tomb for eternity. I was content to rest in place forever.

It was early morning of the third day when I felt vibrations remnant of the earlier earthquake. But this time, it was different. There was another earthquake. What followed, took both the guards and me completely by surprise. An aberration, like never seen before, dropped from out of the sky. It came at me and with little effort whisked me aside. The guards, in total shock, fainted dead away. The harbinger flew up and perched atop me, as if nothing were out of the ordinary.

From my new vantage point, I could see quite clearly into the open tomb. Even after the strange events of that day, I was quite unprepared for what I saw, or didn't see. The tomb was empty; there was no body inside. It seemed that this Jesus, like Joseph, had also given up the tomb! But Jesus had given up the tomb not for another, but for life! He had risen! And because Jesus came back to life, all those who believe will come out of the grave and have eternal life.

My job was not to secure the tomb, but to witness a miracle. But what I have experienced is only the beginning. For like you, I wait in great anticipation for what is to come. Come, Lord Jesus, Amen.

24

Lenten Prayer

Almighty God, we have celebrated with joy the festival of our Lord's resurrection. Graciously help us to show the power of the resurrection in all that we say and do; through your Son, Jesus Christ our Lord, who lives and reigns with you and the Holy Spirit, one God, now and forever. Amen.

Live From
Jerusalem

A Palm Sunday
Drama

John O. Eby

Live From Jerusalem

Characters
Samuel
Miriam
Jacob
Judas
Pharisee 1
Pharisee 2
Jesus
Crowd — nonspeaking parts, a combination of adults and children

(Miriam and Samuel, news anchorpersons, are seated behind a desk on stage)

Samuel: Good morning, this is *Good Morning Israel* broadcasting today live from Jerusalem. It is in the midst of the preparation for Passover and the city is crowded with people. Excitement is especially high this year because of two things. The Romans have scheduled this time to execute three criminals — two notorious thieves and the rebel Barabbas. I am Samuel of Hebron and with me is the lovely Miriam of Magdala. Miriam, tell us of the other event that makes this Passover one to watch.

Miriam: Thank you, Samuel. For the past three years there have been growing reports about an itinerant preacher named Jesus of Nazareth who has been wandering throughout Israel preaching and reportedly healing sick people. Reports are that just a few days ago he even raised a friend of his from the dead. We will have more on this miraculous claim later in the program.

Samuel: Miriam, we have invited you to co-host his show from our sister station in Tiberius because you have some personal insights into this prophet or preacher or whatever he is. Tell us of you own experience with him.

Miriam: I do not have actual firsthand information, but I have seen from very close what this Jesus does with people. My own sister has been a close follower of his.

Samuel: Oh, really! How close?

Miriam: *Very* close. She has been traveling with him and his companions for over two years.

Samuel: What brought her into that company?

Miriam: Well, my sister has always been a bit of a rebel. She was never content to stay home and cook and sew like other girls. She was always roaming around our village and she became involved with some men that used and abused her.

Samuel: Did they prosecute the men?

Miriam: The men? Of course not! But my sister, yes! They caught one of the men with her and they hauled *her* out to the Sanhedrin to be tried!

Samuel: Why her? Why not the man, or men?

Miriam: The assumption of guilt is always on the woman. They naturally assumed that she seduced the man.

Samuel: How does this involve Jesus?

Miriam: After she was convicted by the Sanhedrin, they brought her to Jesus to try to trap him. They pointed out that she had been convicted of adultery and that the punishment was stoning. Then they asked Jesus what should be done. Jesus simply said, "He who is without sin among you should be the one to cast the first stone." One by one they all just left until Jesus was alone with my sister. Then he offered God's forgiveness and told her to change her life.

Samuel: Did she?

Miriam: Did she ever! It was the difference between night and day! She came home, and was reconciled with us all. All that rebellion was gone and a sweet, warm glow surrounded her. Then she asked our mother and father permission to go with Jesus. My parents were so thrilled with the transformation they saw that they gave her permission *and their blessing*!

Samuel: So she has been traveling with Jesus ever since?

Miriam: Yes, mostly in the Galilee area. She comes home frequently and shares what she has seen Jesus do and what she has heard him say.

Samuel: What about the miracles? There have been reports of people blind from birth receiving sight, of lame persons leaping from their beds, of lepers being cleansed, demons cast out, even people being raised from the dead. What does she say about all these? Are they genuine?

Miriam: She swears they all are very, very real and true reports! She saw many of those firsthand. She even saw Jesus feed 5,000 people with only two fish and five loaves of bread.

Samuel: The temple leaders have sent out an order that anyone who sees Jesus should report his presence so he could be arrested. Does your sister think Jesus will come to the Passover celebration amongst all these threats?

Miriam: Well, she is here! So is Jesus' mother and all his close followers! None of them knows for sure because Jesus went off into the wilderness by himself. But they are all here! They are all expecting him to come.

Samuel: This could turn into a real riot with all of Jesus' followers here and the Sanhedrin determined to arrest him. The tension is already high with the Romans planning an execution during the Holy Days of Passover. Will the followers of Jesus fight back if Jesus is arrested?

Miriam: Not likely. Not if they have listened to Jesus. He has forbidden violence. But some of his followers are real hot heads — Peter and James and John, tough fishermen from Capernaum, and one to really watch is Simon. He was a Zealot before he began to follow Jesus.

Samuel: A Zealot? One of those terrorists? What is Jesus doing with a terrorist in his bunch?

Miriam: You would never believe Simon was *ever* a terrorist! The change is amazing! And James and John, well, even Jesus jokes with them about being "Sons of Thunder." But John particularly has become one of the most gentle, loving guys.

Samuel: Careful there, Miriam! You are letting your bias show and we reporters are supposed to stay objective.

Miriam: I am not saying I *believe* all this ... just that my sister is *totally* convinced and I have certainly seen the change in *her*! So *something* is happening in all this.

Samuel: Wait, we have some news coming in from the field. Jacob, can you hear me? Where are you and what is going on?

(Crowd begins to talk and sing and shout in foyer. Jacob and Judas are offstage)

Jacob: Yes, I hear you Samuel. But the noise around me is loud, so pardon me if I do not hear all you ask.

Samuel: What is going on? Where are you?

Jacob: Right now I am in Bethany, just over the Mount of Olives from Jerusalem. We came here because a lot of people had gathered to see Lazarus, the man that reportedly Jesus raised from the dead.

Samuel: What is all the noise about?

Jacob: There have been reports that Jesus is here, too. There! Over there! Scan the camera over there. The crowd is particularly thick. I think he may be in the midst of that crowd.

Samuel: We can see on our monitor, but it does not seem to be projecting to the audience.

Jacob: There, yes, that man you see right there, the man on the left, is Lazarus, the man they say was dead ... and there are his sisters, Martha and Mary. I interviewed them earlier.

Miriam: Look, that woman just to the right of that donkey. That is my sister ... and that big guy, that is Peter. I met him once. Not especially handsome, but strong as an ox.

Samuel: Jacob, what else do you see? Can you get in a little closer to Jesus?

Jacob: I'm not sure! The crowd is really packed in. Oh, Sir, Sir? Can I ask you a couple of questions? Aren't you one of Jesus' followers?

Judas: Yes, I am Judas Iscariot. I have been with Jesus for three years.

Jacob: What do you think Jesus will do? Will he try to go to Jerusalem?

Judas: Oh, yes! He is the Messiah! He is going to ride into Jerusalem and become *king*!

Jacob: But where are his armies, his chariots? Who is going to make him king, this bunch of people?

Judas: Yes, this bunch of people and the power of God! Listen to what they are shouting. They are repeating the Messianic Psalms of David, the Hallel! "Blessed is he who comes in the name of the Lord ... Hosanna, Lord, save us, we pray thee!"

Jacob: Would these common people fight?

Judas: These crowds are ready to *fight and die* for Jesus!

Jacob: But against the whole Roman army? And against the temple guard *both*?

Judas: Ever hear of David and Goliath? Joshua and Jericho? Hezekiah and the Assyrian army? God is at work! It will be *God's* power!

Jacob: How can you be so sure?

Judas: Look at the signs! The prophets said the Messiah would come riding a donkey over the Mount of Olives. The prophets predicted that the people would wave palm branches and would shout out the Hallel! Our religious leaders have long said that as the Messiah rides toward Jerusalem the dead will rise! Look who is here — Lazarus — and that boy with his mother over there — see right there! Do you know who that is? That is the boy from Nain that Jesus raised from the dead. And there! That man in fancy clothes — that is Jairus, the synagogue leader. The little girl with him was dead and Jesus raised *her* from the dead! Nobody since Elijah and Elisha has raised the dead! I tell you, Jesus is going into Jerusalem to be crowned *king*! Look! The crowds are moving. I'm outta here! I do not want to miss *this*!

Jacob: Samuel, Miriam! I am going to try to keep up! I will tune in when I can, but ... over and out.

Samuel: There you have it, folks! We are looking east at the Mount of Olives.

Miriam: Look, there they come! They're cresting the top of the Mount of Olives.

(Crowd enters down all aisles — composed of singing and dancing children and adults — enter with Jesus in the center)

Samuel: Crowds of them.

Miriam: We can hear them all the way down here.

(Procession continues)

Miriam: There is Jesus in the midst of the crowd.

Samuel: They are winding their way past the tombs and gravestones that cover this part of the Mount of Olives.

Miriam: Jesus is near that grove of olives. I understand this is one of his favorite places to come to pray.

Samuel: What is he doing? Jacob, are you there? What is Jesus doing?

Jacob: I hear you, Samuel. Jesus has stopped. Some of the Pharisees have come and mingled in the crowd. They are trying to talk to Jesus. They seem angry. Let me see if I can get in closer to hear what they are saying.

Pharisee 1: Jesus, do you hear what these people are saying?

Pharisee 2: They are calling you the Messiah! King of the Jews!

Pharisee 1: Stop them! Don't you realize that is dangerous? If the Romans see and hear all this they will be up here with force! They will take over the temple area.

Jesus: I tell you, if they kept quiet, the very stones would start shouting!

(Pharisees turn and walk away angrily)

Jacob: Sir, Sir, I heard your interchange with Jesus. What do you think is going to happen?

Pharisee 2: He is a menace! He is a danger to us all! He *has* to be stopped!

(Pharisees exit)

Jacob: Samuel, Miriam, I am going to try to work my way closer to Jesus. He seems to be upset, perhaps even weeping.

Samuel: Yes, get in as close as you can.

Jacob: Excuse me, excuse me ... *(in a "golf tournament announcer" low voice)* Jesus is weeping and, I think, praying.

Jesus: Oh, Jerusalem, Jerusalem. If you only knew today what is needed for peace! But now you cannot see it! You kill the prophets and stone the messengers God has sent you! How many times I wanted to put my arms around all your people, just as a hen gathers her chicks under her wings, but you would not let me! So your enemies will destroy you and your temple will be abandoned and empty because you did not recognize the time when God came to save you.

Miriam: Did you hear that? Jesus is saying that Jerusalem and the temple will be destroyed.

Samuel: Did I ever! That is a bold prophecy! Look, they are on the move again.

Miriam: They have come through the gates of Jerusalem and are entering the temple area.

Samuel: Jacob, can you fill us in on what is happening? The crowd is right below us now.

Jesus: *(As he overturns the tables of the moneychangers)* Get out of here! It is written in the scriptures that God's house should be a house of prayer, but you have made it a den of thieves!

(The merchants run out. The crowd falls back, shocked at the outburst)

Judas: *(Off to the side)* Yes, yes, it has begun! The rebellion has begun.

(After a long pause, Jesus turns, looks at the people, opens his arms and speaks)

Jesus: Come to me, all you who labor and are heavy laden and I will give you rest. Take my yoke and put it on you and learn from me, because I have come to bring peace. My yoke is easy and my burden is light. And you shall have rest for your souls.

(The people hesitate for a second, but immediately the two children who have been raised from the dead rush into the arms of Jesus. Then the crowd does the same)

Jacob: I should be saying something, but nothing seems appropriate. The people are embracing their Messiah. But this is certainly not what I had imagined. This Jesus is *not* a man of war and rebellion. He has come for some other purpose. He is obviously not out to get power or position, but the people love him. They love him ... and he loves them with a gentle, tender love.

(Jesus exits with the crowd)

Samuel: What do you think, Miriam? This conflict between Jesus and the Pharisees and merchants is intense.

Miriam: And this is only the first day of the Passover week.

Samuel: Do you think there will be a rebellion?

Miriam: No, no rebellion. This Jesus would never stand for that. My sister says exactly what Jacob was remarking about. This Jesus is a man of peace, a man who shows great love for God and for the people. He will not lead a rebellion, and he will not allow one to be led in his name.

Samuel: But what, then? What will happen these next six days?

Miriam: I am not sure. I guess we will all have to wait and see.

Samuel: This is Samuel of Hebron and Miriam of Magdala. Tune in tomorrow for an update. And this had been *Good Morning Israel*.

Maundy Thursday
Testimonies

A Series Of Dramatic Readings
For Four Speakers

David H. Covington

Maundy Thursday Testimonies

This series of dramatic readings is to be used as part of a Maundy Thursday service. Note that each speaker speaks twice, with the order of speaking reversed the second time.

Appropriate musical pieces (choral or instrumental) should be used to separate each character's testimony, or at least the two statements made by Peter, since each statement is presented from a different perspective.

Mary: I am Mary from Magdala in Galilee. People say I had fits, had demons. I would fall down and I remember that nothing helped. Eventually, I moved to this city, where I fell in a different way, into a bad way of life. I lost all hope.

Then — I remember the first time I saw him. I was overcome. I don't know why, even now. I couldn't help myself. I started to cry. I hadn't cried in a long, long time. I made a spectacle of myself, really.

It was at the house of Simon — the Pharisee, not the Rock — people everywhere, and in the middle there he was. I burst into tears. I fell at his feet. I felt such a release, a letting go. I poured oil on his feet and rubbed it in with my hair.

Simon — the Pharisee, not the Rock — was irate, but Jesus told him why I was. He said I loved him more because he had forgiven me more.

And he had. I had done so many foolish things, so many bad things, made so many bad choices, and — he forgave me. I was loved, for me, no matter what I had done.

I followed him from that day forward.

Now — I am lost again. We are lost. He's gone. Dead. We — we had hope. I had hope. For the first time. And now. What will we do?

Thomas: I am Thomas, the twin.

Well, it's over. What will we do now? No one knows.

Too much has happened. None of it makes sense.

I never understood the rituals. All this dunking and sprinkling and washing. This laying on of hands and speaking in riddles. I wanted things to be clear, things called by their proper names, no dancing about. I tried to make sense of it. I wanted to know the plan, wanted to know where we were going.

I don't understand anything anymore. Everything is upside down.

On Sunday we're the talk of Jerusalem. Our expectations are grand, suddenly, after all the confusing time on the journey. By Thursday Jesus is talking about betrayals and farewells. Then Judas — the unspeakable traitor! — Judas sells us out.

Judas: I am Judas from Kerioth in Judah. I settle my accounts. I keep track of things, count money, make budgets, figure the cost, calculate the risk.

I cannot abide waste — oil squandered on an anointing, opportunities for advancement missed — I *invested* in the man, don't you see? Gave him my time, my expertise — I saw promise. There was a future here. We had a chance to become — well, there was no limit. Potential return on investment — 100 — no — 1,000 percent.

But he insisted — insisted on throwing it away. I felt cheated. Bitter? Yes, I was bitter as vinegar. All that effort, all those plans. Gone to dust.

And those "disciples." Fools, every one. Incompetents and sycophants. Hanging on his every word, but not understanding a single one. Let's see how they get along without him now. Peter the Rock, indeed. More like an impetuous clod of dirt. And Mary. Always hanging about. Every time I turn around, she's anointing him! The others, too. Fools, I say.

I grew disillusioned. He wouldn't listen to me. What's the use giving unheeded advice? I grant you, he had a way about him, and some marketable skills. He could make them stand up and walk, all right. But he wouldn't charge for it. Never took gifts from the grateful. Missing chances to take hold, to make something of himself.

And this latest. He lets the woman — that woman — pour a fortune of oil over him — a year's wages! — and then he kills any chance of a deal with the temple priests — we could have had a cut of that concession if we'd played it right!

It grew time to settle accounts. I always get a return on my investments. One way or the other.

Peter: Yes, I'm Peter. I'll admit it now — now that it's too late. I wish I had died with him. I wish I had died *instead* of him.

Who am I kidding? I said I didn't know him. I ran away. I hid. I was so scared. Some Rock.

I could kill the traitor Judas, that bean counter. What's the use? It's too late. And I am no better than he. We all allowed this to happen. Why didn't we see it coming?

He did. That supper two nights ago. He washed our feet, and said we were to remember him. Who could forget it? But what is there to remember? What can we do now?

Musical interlude

Peter: Then they put him on the cross. It was about nine in the morning, after we had been up all night, running all over Jerusalem, hearing rumors, hiding. Confusion.

We heard he was to be crucified.

The crowd was huge, even at that hour of the morning. Word had spread among the people. Everybody wanted to see. I stayed well back, in the crowd. I couldn't see well. Couldn't hear anything but hawkers and dogs and restless children. Morning conversations from sleepy Passover crowds.

A shout went up when the nails went home. A carpenter's son joined to the wood. And then I saw the tops of the crosses above the crowd, up on the hill, the place of skulls.

I couldn't stay there anymore. It was too much. I wandered through the streets and tried to think. I couldn't think. I was so tired. I was so alone. How could I have left him in his hour of need? And now it's too late.

Judas: I went to see the account closed.

The trial had been rougher than I had imagined. He didn't say anything — or anything much — in his defense. "Are you the Messiah?" he was asked. "You say that I am," he answered. He didn't bother to answer the other questions.

I gave my testimony, and it was well received. I told only the truth, no more and no less. The man got beyond himself, and he broke the law, and he deserved to be punished. I am not sorry. I am not sorry.

I had a good view of the crucifixion. Guest of honor, you might say. I must admit he took it well. He touched me, almost, the way he suffered. He even looked my way once. He didn't say anything. But those eyes!

I didn't expect that.

I began to rethink this.

Thomas: It was a long day. About noon it got dark when the clouds rolled over. No one thought anything of it — just shade from the sun. The thunder growled and once or twice I thought the earth trembled, but the crowd had nowhere to go.

I wanted to see. I got up close, pushed my way to the front. I stepped on a few toes along the way, believe me. When I got there, I wished I hadn't. I saw the soldiers hammer the spikes home, heard him bark with the pain, saw the blood, and smelled the intensity of the crowd. When the soldiers raised the cross to set it upright, he cried out again with the pain — but when they offered him the drugged wine to blunt the pain, he refused. He was filthy, and the dogs were running among the crosses, his and the other two. The soldiers laughed and gambled and ignored him. The crowd yelled insults.

By three, it was done. We had a storm then, and we all got soaked. Some of us wept, too.

Mary: He changed my life. He loved me. He showed me that all people might love each other. His death has left me empty.

I tried to hide my weeping.

What did he think about as he was hanging there for those six hours? His life? The decisions he had made? The failings of his followers? His terror and anguish? Or some mystery, some dream of holiness?

I am going to anoint his body one last time. It's the least I can do. But, oh! It's the most I can do, too.

I must be careful. There are soldiers about!

God On Trial,
Or...?

A Good Friday
Drama

John O. Eby

God On Trial, Or...?

Characters
Pilate
Beelzebub
Johannis
Jesus
Nicodemus
Isaac
Peter
Caiaphas
Judas

Jesus is on trial before Pilate. Beelzebub is the prosecutor, presenting witnesses with various accusations against Jesus. Jesus is defending himself.

(A courtroom setting. Pilate is seated in the center of the stage, behind a desk. Witnesses will come to a witness stand at Pilate's left. Jesus is seated at the right of the room and Beelzebub is seated to the left. Both are seated at tables)

Pilate: Order in the court. Prosecutor Beelzebub, would you call your first witness?

Beelzebub: Your Honor, my first witness is Johannis of Jerusalem.

(Johannis takes the witness stand)

Beelzebub: Please, state your full name.

Johannis: Johannis of Jerusalem.

Beelzebub: What is your occupation?

Johannis: I am a prominent member of Herod's court. I am responsible for overseeing the finances in Herod's kingdom.

Beelzebub: What is your charge against the defendant, Jesus of Nazareth?

Johannis: He makes himself out to be a leader, but he is totally irresponsible. He would destroy the financial framework and security of our country.

Beelzebub: Please explain what you personally have seen him do or say.

Johannis: I was willing to be one of his followers. He is charismatic. He is compassionate. He is the kind of leader I thought we needed. So I went to him and volunteered to become part of his party. He said to me, "Go. Sell all you have and give it to the poor. Then come and follow me."

Beelzebub: And that frightened you?

Johannis: Of course! Imagine the chaos if people followed that advice! Who would run our businesses? Who would raise our crops? Who would manage all the land? Poor people could not do that! They are poor because they cannot manage anything! If people did what Jesus expects from them, there would be utter chaos in our society. We need a more businesslike approach.

Jesus: Father, forgive him. He does not know what he is saying.

(Johannis leaves the witness stand)

Pilate: Prosecutor Beelzebub, call your next witness.

Beelzebub: Your honor, I call Nicodemus to the stand.

(Nicodemus takes the witness stand)

Beelzebub: Please state your full name and occupation.

Nicodemus: My name is Nicodemus. I am a member of the Sanhedrin.

Beelzebub: And what is your charge against the defendant, Jesus of Nazareth?

Nicodemus: Sir, I really do not have a charge against him.

Beelzebub: Your honor, permission to treat this witness as a hostile witness.

Pilate: So ordered.

Beelzebub: Have you been a part of all the discussions of the Sanhedrin about the defendant?

Nicodemus: Yes, Sir. I have.

Beelzebub: Has the defendant called you "whitewashed tombs" and "hypocrites"?

Nicodemus: Yes, Sir. He has! But he was right! We at times have been just that — hypocrites.

Beelzebub: Your honor, I move to strike that comment.

Pilate: So ordered. Witness is instructed to only answer the question.

Beelzebub: Mr. Nicodemus, are you a secret follower of Jesus?

Nicodemus: Your honor, I plead the Fifth Amendment. I refuse to answer on grounds that the evidence may incriminate me.

Beelzebub: Hah! You are afraid of being associated with Jesus.

Jesus: Father, please forgive him. He does not realize what he is doing.

(Nicodemus leaves the witness stand)

Pilate: Prosecution, call your next witness.

Beelzebub: My next witness, your honor, is Isaac of Nazareth.

(Isaac takes the witness stand)

Beelzebub: Please, state your full name and occupation.

Isaac: My name is Isaac of Nazareth. I am a stonemason.

Beelzebub: And what is your testimony?

Isaac: Jesus said he was going to destroy the temple!

Beelzebub: That is sacrilege! That is treason. That would cause a riot, a civil war!

Pilate: Prosecutor, save it for your summation. Ask the question you want to ask.

Beelzebub: Sir, did the defendant say *how* he would destroy the temple?

Isaac: No, he just said that he would destroy it and rebuild it in three days.

Pilate: Rebuild it in three days?

Beelzebub: Your honor, I move to have that statement stricken. It was not in the testimony he shared with me.

Pilate: Declined. That statement is pertinent. Sir, tell me again. What exactly did you hear this defendant say?

Isaac: Well, as I recall it was something like "I will destroy this temple and I will raise it again in three days."

Pilate: You are absolutely sure that is what you heard? He said, "I *will* destroy the temple"?

Isaac: Pretty sure. There was a lot of confusion and noise that day. The *last* part of it I am absolutely sure about, the first part I heard but was not entirely focused on what he was saying.

Pilate: So you are not sure that he was threatening violence or not.

Isaac: Not for certain for certain, but it did *sound* threatening!

Jesus: Father, forgive him. He is not sure what he is saying.

(Isaac leaves the witness stand)

Pilate: Prosecutor, you had better call your next witness.

Beelzebub: Your honor, I call Peter of Capernaum. And your honor, since it is alleged that he is one of Jesus' closest followers I request permission to treat him as a hostile witness.

Pilate: Permission granted.

(Peter takes the witness stand)

Beelzebub: State your name and occupation.

Peter: Peter of Capernaum, fisherman.

Beelzebub: I understand that you are one of the defendant's followers. Is this true?

Peter: *(Pauses)* No.

Pilate: You will have to speak up. Are you one of the followers of the defendant, Jesus of Nazareth?

Peter: No.

Beelzebub: You do not know this defendant, Jesus of Nazareth?

Peter: *No!* I do not know him!

Beelzebub: Your honor, this witness is *lying*! He has perjured himself.

Pilate: Prosecutor, do you have any other questions you want to ask this witness?

Beelzebub: Your honor, he has destroyed his credibility with his lies. I had *much* I wanted to ask him, but it was contingent upon his telling us the truth about his relationship with the defendant!

Pilate: The witness is dismissed.

Jesus: Father, please forgive him. He does not realize what he has just done.

(Peter leaves the witness stand)

Pilate: Do you have any more witnesses?

Beelzebub: Your honor, I call Caiaphas to the stand.

(Caiaphas takes the witness stand)

Beelzebub: Please state your name and your occupation.

Caiaphas: Caiaphas of Jerusalem, currently I am serving as high priest.

Beelzebub: As high priest do you have any special concerns about the defendant?

Caiaphas: I most certainly do. He teaches that he is God in the flesh! That is blasphemy.

Beelzebub: Blasphemy! That is the most serious of all crimes.

Caiaphas: Absolutely!

Beelzebub: And what is the penalty for this crime?

Caiaphas: According to the Torah, the penalty for blasphemy is death.

Pilate: Mr. Prosecutor, this is a civil court, not a religious court. The defendant is being judged by Roman law, not because of any religious doctrine.

Beelzebub: But your honor, to these people this is an issue of *supreme* importance. The Roman government has allowed the Sanhedrin much authority in self-governance.

Pilate: True, but the Roman law overrides all these local rules, especially religious ones. What are the *civil* charges against this defendant?

Beelzebub: Well, ah ... disturbing the peace, ah, threatening the security of the people ... ah ... undermining the authority of the very Sanhedrin that your government recognizes.

Pilate: Help me out here a little. It is my position to maintain peace in this part of the world, so I am on your side in that. But I have to abide by Roman law. I have to have more justification than some vague claims that the peace of mind of a few Sanhedrin members is being threatened. What has this man done that he deserves to be on trial today? Is he a terrorist? Does he advocate the violent overthrow of the Roman government? Is he gathering a hidden army so he can proclaim himself king?

Beelzebub: Ah ... yes! Yes, that is it! This man claims to be the King of the Jews!

Pilate: Jesus of Nazareth, is this true? Are you the King of the Jews?

Jesus: Yes, it is as you have said. But my kingdom is not of this world. If it were, my followers would fight. But my kingdom is *not* of this world.

Pilate: Mr. Prosecutor, Mr. Caiaphas. I cannot try this man. You have brought me nothing with which I can charge or convict this man. You helped us catch that terrorist Barabbas last week and we had *plenty* of evidence on him — weapons, witnesses, victims of his crimes — give me even a *little* of that, even a little, and I will keep this guy locked up until my term here is over.

But wait, here is a solution. It has been my custom since I have been governor to allow you to choose one prisoner to be set free during your holy Passover time. Here, Mr. Caiaphas, is your choice. You may choose Barabbas or the defendant, this Jesus of Nazareth. Which would you have me set free?

Caiaphas: Barabbas!

Pilate: Barabbas? He has killed and robbed some of your own people! I have yet to hear one iota of evidence that the defendant has done ANYTHING to hurt anyone, except to threaten your grip on power. You want me to release Barabbas? Ah, well, so be it. Guards, release Barabbas.

Jesus: Father, forgive them. They really do not understand what they are doing.

(Caiaphas leaves the witness stand)

Beelzebub: Your honor, we have one more witness. He has the best evidence yet!

Pilate: I certainly hope so. Call in your next witness.

Beelzebub: Your honor, I call Judas Iscariot.

(Judas takes the witness stand)

Beelzebub: State your name and occupation.

Judas: My name is Judas Iscariot. I am a follower of Jesus.

Pilate: Is that your occupation?

Judas: Well, currently I am unemployed. I just follow Jesus. But I *am* the treasurer of the group.

Pilate: Proceed.

Beelzebub: Judas, as a follower of Jesus, what have you observed or seen him do?

Judas: Oh, lots of things — healing the sick, feeding the hungry, teaching, lots of teaching. I even saw him raise a dead man.

Beelzebub: No, that is not what I mean. What have you seen him do or heard him say that is an act of a criminal?

Judas: False hope! He gives people false hope! The people want a Messiah and he claims to be one, but he will not allow them to fight. The people want someone to throw out the ... oops. The people want someone who will be a king and all he offers is parables. The people want a strong authority and all he does is wash their feet and feed them. *False hope!* False hope! That is what he is guilty of!

Pilate: That's it? That is your best evidence? You have not convinced me of anything! The defendant is guilty of nothing illegal.

Beelzebub: You cannot turn him loose. There will be riots, chaos. Those always spill over until you have to unleash the power of the Roman government on the masses. That results in more riots and chaos. Your honor, you cannot release this man!

Pilate: What would you have me do with him then?

Beelzebub: Crucify him! Crucify him! Call him a rebel. After all he DID say he was King of the Jews! Call him a traitor. Crucify him as an example of what will happen to anyone who calls himself King of the Jews!

Pilate: Hmmm! Yes, that will work. Guards! Take the defendant. Prepare a cross for him. Make sure the sign above his head is in every language so the people will read, "This is the King of the Jews."

Jesus: Father, forgive them all. They really do not understand at all what they are doing!

Sons Of Thunder

A Good Friday
Drama

Carol Secord

Sons Of Thunder

Characters
    John
    Mary
    James

(John and Mary walk upstairs to platform. They walk as if weighted by their sorrow. They pause at Mary's "door," in front of a wooden bench)

Mary: Thank you, John. *(Shakes her head in disappointment about the others)* You're the only one ... who stayed.

John: I will do what he said, Mary. I'll be your son, and take care of you just as *(Voice breaks)* he would have done himself.

Mary: I know you will. *(Looks at John)* I still think I'm going to see him, somehow, as if none of this really happened. I half expect him to walk over and shake his head at me for not understanding, *again.*

John: *(In a strangled voice)* There's a lot I don't understand. He tried to tell us so many things, these last few days ... I can't even remember what all he said, much less what it meant. *(With pent-up anger)* If only I could understand *why* this had to happen. *(Looks down, trying to conceal his tears)*

Mary: *(Gently blots his tears, speaks softly)* When you understand ... will you tell me?

John: *(Hoarsely, looks in Mary's face)* You will be the first, Mother.

(Mary touches John's cheek with her hand and wipes away his tears. He puts his hands on her forearms in both pledge and care. They exchange a mournful gaze, then Mary turns and trudges through the door on the pulpit side. John paces fretfully, leans against a wall and suddenly pounds it with his fist. He turns his face upward in anguish and cries out in anger against Jesus for abandoning his little band of believers)

John: *Why* did you have to die? How could you leave us like this? You promised to make us fishers of men — but you let yourself get caught in the Pharisees' nets! And for what? What? *(Strides around the platform like a caged animal. Occasionally, he raises his arms in as he rails at Jesus)*

It just doesn't make any sense to me. What was all this for, anyway? Why go to the trouble? Why did you heal those sick people and spend all that time preaching, just to be hung on a cross like a common criminal? *(Ends of up front of the bench. Pounds a fist into his other hand, glares heavenward, demanding an answer)*

I want to know *why!* *(Settles into the bench with a heavy sigh. He looks heavenward, then leans his arms against his thighs and buries his face in his hands. He shakes with sobs)*

(James enters furtively from side aisle near pulpit. He's been looking for John while trying to evade the Pharisees and Roman soldiers. He sees John, approaches joyfully at first, then, hesitantly, unsure of how John will receive him. James walks up the steps, stands to one side of the bench. John, his face down, still does not see James)

James: John?

(John slowly raises his head from his hands. He looks at James with no expression)

James: *(Approaches slowly)* It's ... over?

John: *(Bitterly)* Yes, "It is finished." Those were his final words, James. But, you wouldn't know that, would you? You and all the others ran off the minute Judas came with the temple guards. *(Turns away from James)*

James: *(His quick temper flares)* There you go again! All my life you've thought you were the best — and then told me about it over and over again. *(Kicks at unseen trash on the ground)* Maybe you need to have a little sense knocked into you! Those guards would've taken in every one of us as traitors, and had us killed, too.

John: *(Antagonized)* I was *there*, James. You, and Peter, and all the rest ... *weren't*. Nowhere to be found. Gone. Van ...

James: *(Cuts John off)* I get the picture. You weren't exactly out in the open, though, were you? So don't brag to me about being the only one with him! *(Aggressively leans toward John's face and shoves his shoulder)*

(John jumps up, shoves James. James responds. Just as the scuffle seems about to escalate into a fist fight, John shakes his head as if in pain, makes a dismissing gesture and sits back down)

John: *(His voice is hollow, defeated)* It's not worth fighting about. For the first time in my life, I don't feel like fighting about anything. I just ... hurt. *(Sinks back into the bench, ignoring James)*

(James props one leg on opposite end of the bench and leans over. They remain in silence for a long moment. John again lowers his head into his hands)

James: Y'know, John, this isn't like anything else we've been through. We really need to pull together.

John: *(Doesn't answer for a moment, then looks up with a mournful grin)* I guess even the "Sons of Thunder" could stop thundering and ... act like brothers. *(Stands with his arms stretched toward James)*

(James stands, and they embrace. They both weep for Christ. They pull apart, wiping their tears, and sit back down on the bench)

James: It must've been awful, watching him ... die.

John: *(Nods, tortured by the memory)* Trust the Romans to come up with the most horrible way to kill a man. *(Pauses, overcome by grief and anger. His voice is choked when he resumes)* When the soldier thrust that spear into his side, and the water gushed out, I knew it was over ... I've never known darkness that black. Never. *(Shakes his head and sighs deeply)*

James: But, how did the Romans even get involved? What do they care about Jesus? All his arguments were with the Pharisees.

John: Oh, but our great high priest told the council that if they didn't do something about Jesus, the Romans would take away the power of the council. *(Shakes his head miserably)* They've been looking for an excuse to kill him ever since he raised Lazarus from the dead.

James: *(Grimly)* And Judas gave them exactly what they needed.

John: *(Anger boils up again)* Ahhh, that *traitor.* I never understood why Jesus invited him to join the group. And Jesus knew Judas was going to betray him, James. He said so at our Passover meal. *(Furious with himself for not acting on the knowledge, with Judas for his betrayal, and with Jesus for letting it happen)*
I should've killed the coward on the spot. Why did I just let him walk out when Jesus said, "What you do, do quickly." None of this had to happen! Hmmm. Where *is* Judas?

James: I've heard he went back to the priests, and they laughed at him. No one's really seen him since that night in the garden.

John: And they won't, if I see him first. How about that other traitor, Peter? *(Mocking tone of voice)* "The Rock," who denied that he even *knew* Jesus?

James: Well, we all found each other, eventually, and we've been together in the room where we had Passover. Peter came later, but he won't say anything to anyone, or eat, or do anything but stare at the wall and *(Hesitates, uncertain whether to tell John)* ... sometimes cry.

John: Is he there now? I'll rip his heart out for denying he knew Jesus!

James: *(Pulls on John's arm)* Hey, slow down. We all need each other, even more now that Jesus is gone. *(Leans toward John, speaks confidentially)* Believe me, Peter is suffering a lot, reliving what he did. If you killed him, you'd just relieve his pain.

John: *(Grimly)* I wouldn't want to do that. Let him suffer. *(Turns to James)* Y'know, I can't take any more of this. All these things we can't understand, all the sorrow. Let's go back to the boats, James, to do what we *know.* Father never understood why we just walked off and left the business, we could ...

James: *(Touches John's arm)* Maybe in a few days. Right now, well, I think the others need to hear what you have to say.

John: *(Stubbornly)* They could've been there, too.

James: *(Impatience flares)* But we weren't, John. *(His tone and demeanor soften)* For whatever reasons, we weren't. And if Jesus taught us anything at all, it was to love one another, just the way he loved us ... *(Emphasizes)* Jesus would show compassion.

John: *(Looks at James ruefully)* I wish you hadn't listened to him so well.

James: *(He's grasped a concept that eludes many Christians, says with a little smile)* I did, though, and although there are lots of things I don't understand about what's happened, or why, I do know what Jesus wants us to do — right now.

(James stands and walks a few steps, while John sits. James turns and holds out his arm. John stands; they embrace and walk up the aisle together)

The Animals Learn
The Meaning
Of Easter

A Children's
Easter Play

Will Rabert

To my wife, Martha,
whose experience with preschool, kindergarten, and special children,
and the mothering of our own three children,
taught me how to relate to children

The Animals Learn The Meaning Of Easter

Characters (15 speaking parts)
Narrator
Rabbit
Donkey
Fox
Deer
Bear
Mouse
Dog
Cat
Dove
Owl
Robin
Turkey
Rooster
Hen
Stars
Trees

Small children who can't read or learn speaking parts can be trees or stars. The rest will have cardboard ears or paper plate masks to represent the animal or bird they are portraying. The trees can hold leaves and the stars can hold cut out stars, sprinkled with silver glitter over glue.

Setting
A woods

Narrator: I will read the Easter story from chapter 16 of Mark's Gospel.

(After the reading, the Narrator will announce an Easter hymn. Children enter as the hymn is being sung)

Narrator: It is early Easter morning after sunrise at the edge of the woods and the animals are talking about why the day is special. The animals seem disturbed and a great deal of discussion has been taking place among them. Let's listen and see if we can discover what is bothering them.

Mouse: I don't like how the cat is looking at me. Will you stop licking your mouth everytime you see me?

Cat: I can't help it. Cats like mice, and I'm very hungry.

Bear: You think you are hungry? I've been sleeping all winter. When I came out of my den, I expected to go looking for food. Instead, I have to come to this meeting. What's it all about anyway?

Dog: I called all of us together because the children in my house have been busy all week coloring boiled eggs, and last night they were so excited, I though they'd never get to sleep.

Bear: Who cares what humans do or think, just so they leave us alone. Besides, I'm too hungry to worry about children and their parents.

Cat: *(Still looking at Mouse)* Well, I care. The children are important to me because they play with me, and the grownups feed me.

Mouse: Did they feed you this morning?

Cat: No, that's why I'm hungry.

Mouse: I was afraid of that. Is anyone going to make that cat stop looking at me and licking its mouth? Cats make me nervous.

Dog: Cat, stop it right now. We're all hungry and I don't want us to make one another frightened. We have important business here.

Fox: What can be more important than getting food, not only for us but for our babies? I have four kits in the den waiting for me to bring them something to eat.

Bear: If all of you are going to talk about food and eating, I'm leaving this silly meeting and going to get something for my belly.

Dog: If you'll all be quiet a minute, I'll explain why we're here. Something important is going on today. Did any of you see how people were dressed up in new clothes this morning?

Donkey: We know. Humans are acting strangely and you want to know why. Well, I think humans always act strangely, not quiet and well behaved like us animals.

Robin: You forgot us birds. We're better behaved than the rest of you animals. Besides, you bray so loud, no one would think you are quiet.

(Several animals and birds shout, "Yes," while others shout, "Quiet")

Dog: We have to understand humans. True, the cat and I are the only ones who live with them, but like it or not, humans affect all of us.

Rabbit: Can I say something? Make this meeting short. The fox is looking at me like the cat looks at the mouse. I'm not hungry as I ate some green, tender grass on my way here, but like all of you I have babies in my rabbit hole to feed. The sooner we listen to dog, the sooner we all get out of here and back to our babies and homes.

Dog: Thanks, Rabbit, for being so helpful. I won't chase you as much anymore — *(Pauses)* at least today. Now if we can get back to business. What's so special about this day that humans spent all week busying themselves — cleaning, cooking special food —

Bear: *(Quickly interrupts)* Will you all stop talking about food?

Dog: Sorry. Anyway, my human family, Cat's and mine, are almost as busy as they are at Thanksgiving or Christmas.

Turkey: Don't talk about Thanksgiving. My uncle Joe was on their Thanksgiving table last year – and not as an invited guest.

Hen: Well, I'm interested in what all the human activity is about. They took all the eggs we chickens laid all week, and they didn't eat them for breakfast. They hard boiled them. What are they doing with all those eggs?

Cat: Last night the children were coloring them, and putting pictures on them. They were trying on those new clothes Dog talked about. Then they talked about how today would be Easter.

All except Cat: Easter? What's Easter?

Cat: Well, it can't be Christmas because they just had that a few months ago. Besides, there's no tree and presents.

Dog: It can't be a birthday. We know when everyone in the family has a birthday. But there are baskets filled with candy and small gifts and toys. Too, there were eggs hidden all over the house this morning.

Turkey: As long as it's not Thanksgiving.

Dog: And that's not all. Every basket had a chocolate rabbit in it.

(All look at Rabbit)

Rabbit: Why is everyone looking at me? Oh. No. I'm not the Easter bunny. I've never met him. He's not in my family. We're very nice people, and we don't have anything to do with humans.

Deer: Neither do we. Humans scare us. So, if we can't find out what's special about today to people and why it's called Easter, the deer are leaving, meeting or no meeting.

Dove: I've sat here long enough keeping quiet. If anyone should be able to help us it would be Owl. After all, we all call him the wise old owl.

(All look at Owl)

Owl: Whooooo! I wondered how long you would keep up all the talk and finally get around to me.

Robin: I should have though of asking Owl. We birds are smart. We see how humans act and listen to them talk when we eat the seeds that they put out for us.

All except Owl: Please tell us, Owl.

Owl: If you all keep still and settle down — Cat, get away from Mouse; Fox, get away from Rabbit. Now, as I was saying, if you all keep still and settle down, I'll tell you what my grandfather told me about Easter when I was little.

Dove, Robin, Rooster, Hen, and Turkey: *(One after another)* Please!

Owl: A long, long time ago, so far back we animals and birds couldn't count that far, there was a good man who was Love. He helped people. He healed the sick. He told about God's love for not only humans but the birds and the animals — the whole world.

All except Owl: Ohhh! Please tell us more.

Owl: This man was God's Son. But some people hated him and his talk about love and forgiveness. So they killed him. They hung him on a cross between two thieves, and then they buried him in a tomb.

All except Owl: Ohhh, no!

Owl: But what they didn't know was how much God loves the world and everything he created. God's love is so great that on Sunday, the Son of God, Jesus, rose from the dead and went to heaven to be with his Father. And to this day, people remember God's love on this special day and call it Easter.

Deer: Then you think human beings would remember God's love every day.

Robin: You think they would call every Sunday a special day if Jesus rose on that day of the week.

Mouse: And you think humans would live and love all the time, every day.

Owl: *(Looking at each animal and bird one at a time)* Many do, and yes, there are some who don't know about love. But that is why we animals and birds should be kind and gentle to one another. Maybe when humans see us being good and loving, they will remember Easter every day they live.

Cat: That's a lovely story, Owl. Mouse, I promise you I won't bother you at all today, because it's Easter.

Fox: Rabbit. *(Rabbit looks at Fox)* Me, too. I will leave you alone on this special day.

Owl: Now you know what Easter is all about — *(Pause)* God's love. So happy Easter all of you, and remember God loves you and everything and everyone he created.

Narrator: Yes, Easter is much more than colored eggs, Easter baskets, chocolate rabbits, and new clothes. Easter, as the animals have learned and as we all know, is the day to rejoice because Jesus rose from the dead. And because he rose, he has promised to all who love and believe in him that they, too, will rise and be with God in heaven. Let us rejoice and give thanks to God for Jesus and for Easter.

(Congregation may sing an Easter hymn to close as the children leave)

M.I.H. —
Missing In Heaven

An Easter Sunrise Worship Service
With Children's Story
And Play

Frank Ramirez

M.I.H. (Missing In Heaven) was first presented at the early morning Easter service at Elkhart Valley Church of the Brethren in Elkhart, Indiana, on March 30, 2002.

Thanks to the original cast:
Jane Atkins, Kira Radtke, Dorothy Hill,
Jessica Ramirez, Carolyn Greenwood, Jim Greenwood,
Calley Miller, Jennie Ramirez, Laura Miller

M.I.H. — Missing In Heaven

Easter Sunrise Service

Order Of Worship

Prelude

Call To Worship
   One: Christ is risen. Christ is risen, indeed.
   All: Christ is risen today. Christ lives and reigns.

Unison Invocation
   Jesus, your power is displayed today. We proclaim you are risen and present among us. We proclaim you Lord and Savior. We proclaim your majesty and glory. Bless us in our worship together as we seek to be your disciples of peace and salvation. In your glorious name, we pray. Amen.

Hymn Of Praise   "Low In The Grave He Lay"

Children's Story   "We Know Jesus Is With Us When We're Together"
(Props needed: a loaf of bread or a tray of cookies to share)
   The people who knew Jesus were very sad. Jesus had died on the cross, and his friends saw him buried in the tomb. Two of his friends were walking away from Jerusalem, and they did not know yet what we all know now — that Jesus rose from the dead! He is alive.

   As a matter of fact, Jesus came up and walked with these two friends, but they were so sad they were looking down at the ground. They were so sad they could hardly think. They didn't recognize him.

   But that didn't stop them from visiting with this man they met on the road, the man who was really Jesus. Jesus asked them why they were sad, and they told him it was because Jesus had died. Then Jesus explained the Bible to them, so they would understand that everything that had happened was part of God's plan.

   After a while they came to an inn, and the two friends asked Jesus to stay with them and eat. They still didn't recognize Jesus. It wasn't until Jesus broke the bread so they could share that they realized who was with them! Jesus disappeared, but the friends were so overjoyed they returned to Jerusalem and found out that Jesus had been with their other friends as well.

   Even today, when we gather together in the name of Jesus, and share food with each other, then Jesus is with us again. We may not see Jesus clearly, but he is still risen, he is still alive, and he is still with us when we break bread together.

   Right now we are going to share *(this bread/these cookies)* to remember how Jesus is with us, and to know how good it is to be together when we are all friends of Jesus. Thank you for coming together to share this story.

Joys And Concerns

Morning Prayer

Lord, this day the joys we share are multiplied. Lord, this day even our sorrows are sweet. You have triumphed, Lord, in your resurrection, and as we share in your glory we pledge to live together in your new community, now and in this world, as well as in the next. Bless us, your people, as we pray with the words you taught us, as we say in one voice:

Our Father, who art in heaven, hallowed be thy name. Thy kingdom come, thy will be done on earth as it is in heaven. Give us this day our daily bread, and forgive us our debts as we forgive our debtors. And lead us not into temptation, but deliver us from evil. For thine is the kingdom, the power, and the glory forever. Amen.

Hymn Of Resurrection   "Christ The Lord Is Risen Today"

A Time Of Offering

Scripture   Matthew 28:1-10

Scripture Response   Colossians 3:1
   All: So if you have been raised with Christ, seek the things that are above, where Christ is, seated at the right hand of God.

An Easter Offering   "M.I.H. — Missing In Heaven"

Benediction

Benediction Hymn   "Proclaim The Tidings Near And Far"

Children's Benediction*   "He Is Risen Indeed!"

Benediction Response   "And I Will Raise You Up"

Postlude

*The children are invited to come forward to proclaim this benediction.

M.I.H. — Missing In Heaven

Easter Sunrise Play

Characters
    Angel Gabriel
    Angel Wonderful
    The Bible
    The Star
    The Old Lamb
    The Table
    The Colt
    The Cross
    The Stone

Scene
    Heaven on early Sunday morning, following the original Good Friday

Presentation
    This play was originally presented in the style of Readers' Theater. The parts may be memorized (especially the parts other than the Angels) or read. Costumes may be elaborate, symbolic, or simple.

Note
    The name for the Angel Wonderful came from Judges 13:18, at least as it appears in some translations.

(The two Angels [Gabriel and Wonderful] share one music stand, on which was laid a script. A second music stand is beside it, and the other characters come up one by one to read their individual parts)

Gabriel
I am Gabriel, who stands before God
Reflecting his glory and running about
Performing his errands, and I think it odd
That heaven is empty. I stand here and shout,

"Hey! Where's everybody?" I don't see an angel!
I left for what seemed like a moment or two
To wander through quasars and black holes that mangle
Whole galaxies 'til you see light shining through.

Did I tell you the time that I saw Zechariah
Who shared with his wife a wish for a son?
I told him a child was coming, no lie t'yah,
If I tell you a thing, then it's gonna be done.

71

He said he believed me, but wanted a sign
To demonstrate that all these marvels are nigh t'us.
I gave him a throatful (the idea was mine)
A spectacular nine-month-long laryngitis.

I like to stay busy, so I flew away
To a village called Nazareth in Galilee
To speak with a woman named Mary and say
That she would give birth to a Savior for thee.

Though she was a virgin, this woman named Mary
As Isaiah prophesied ages ago,
For nine months against expectations would carry
Messiah to term — and I told her just so.

Now how would she answer, we angels would wonder,
When asked if she'd take on this task for us all?
She paused and I thought I would just burst asunder
But then she replied that she'd answer the call.

It wasn't long afterward Joseph discovered
That Mary was pregnant before they were wed.
He might have caused trouble. I quietly hovered
And waited until he had gone to his bed.

And then in a dream I told Joe his intended
Was righteous and had by the Spirit conceived
The one who'd forgive sins, as prophets portended.
The carpenter woke and he plainly believed.

You know all the rest. With the census they call
To homeland and hearth the whole family
And whether an Inn or a quaint B & B
No room could be found except in a stall.
That night there was born the king of us all.

The choir of angels told shepherds the news.
We hung up a star so a Magi who views
The heavens would know that a king had been born
In Bethlehem's stable that heavenly morn.

It was only a minute — or could it be years? —
When I flew down to earth to see Joseph and Mary,
And sang to the shepherds, allaying their fears,
I had earned a vacation, and so did not tarry

To see how the whole thing came out when the Lord
In the form of an infant was battling the breeze
With his tiny hands waving, the incarnate Word
Who set the whole world in a blaze with a sneeze!

So where is this Jesus and how do I find him?
I know there's no power below or on earth
Throughout the whole universe strong that could bind him,
No one forever that's matching his worth!

He's missing in heaven, he's missing below.
I've looked for him everywhere, looked high and low.
And no other angel around seems to know.
You there, the one who runs errands, come here.
What have you seen? Can you make this all clear?

Wonderful
You call and I come from my post where I watch
To see all that time and temptation can catch.
From here at the edge of our heaven my eye
Roves forward and backward in hopes I might spy
The doings of he whom the scriptures call Word
But we know much better as Jesus the Lord.
All heaven is buzzing. We look for the Savior
And ponder this awkward and puzzling behavior.
Yes, Jesus is missing, and will he return?
The question is urgent, and we have concern.
We're glad that you're back from your absence of sorts
And welcome you here to the heavenly courts.
I wait for your orders. I hear your commands.
I patiently seek to obey your demands.

Gabriel
Then fly to the north and the south and the west
And when you are through, if the east is the best
Then search out there also, until you can find
The answers to riddles that trouble the mind.
Bring back to us witnesses who might have seen
The puzzling events that on earth there have been.
Fly now. Fly faster. Come back when you're through.
I promise that we will be waiting for you.

Wonderful
I fly now to earth. When at last I return
I'll answer your questions, address your concern.

73

Gabriel
I stand alone waiting, and heaven is quiet.
Too quiet by half, for when normal a riot
Of flying by angels around heaven's throne
Makes all of us dizzy. I'm still here alone.
Ah, there in the distance, returning, I witness
A number of persons of various fitness
To tell us I hope in its fullness the story
Of Jesus who left us and took with him glory.

Wonderful
I'm back as I promised and hope I have found
The answers to all of your questions profound.
Each personage present in one way or other
Was touched by our Jesus. Perhaps all together
We'll learn what has happened. You know your vacation
Left vacant your eminent glorious station.

Gabriel
I see that you've got in your hands the Great Book,
The words from the prophets and psalmist we took
And set up in letters of gold upon pages
Still read by the wise and the willing and sages.

Wonderful
Let all who seek wisdom be silent and ponder
The words that eternally fill us with wonder.

The Bible
I am the book that is known as the Bible.
I'm truthful and honest, and speak without libel.
The things that I tell, you can trust to be true
Three passages give you together a clue.
The first one is coming from Psalm Twenty-two.
"My God," someone's saying, who hangs from a tree,
And cries to the heavens, "Why am I forsaken?"
The Fifty-third chapter, Isaiah, is taken.

Who would believe this? Our own sins he wore
As if they were his, and he silently bore
The wounds of the guilty though he had not sinned.
This strange apprehension I hear on the wind.
At times, we like sheep had all wandered astray
Oppressed and afflicted, not once did he say

A word in defense. I just say what I've seen.
The last of these verses? From Psalm One-eighteen.

The love of the Lord is enduring forever.
And I will fear nothing for nothing can sever
A love that is steadfast. These words I can give —
My pages say, "I shall not die, but shall live!"

Gabriel
The mystery deepens. But who can make clear
The words from the Bible?

Wonderful
Perhaps this star here.

The Star
I am the light known as Bethlehem's star
Who shines from the heavens where all the stars are.
I shone very bright, so bright that it seems
I've grown very weak and the best of my beams
Are dim, very dim. You know this can't please us.
I shine from on high, but I cannot spot Jesus.
So please ask another. I was there at the start,
But my journey is over. I've finished my part.

Wonderful
Here is another I found as I travel
Whose wool is so fine it would never unravel.
You asked who knew Jesus and where he might be.
This one is the lamb from his Nativity.

Gabriel
But he would have seen him so long, long ago.

Wonderful
He saw him more recently. Thought you should know.

Gabriel
I should have known better. You always come through.
Please tell me the things that you know or you knew.

The Old Lamb
(Enters on a pair of crutches)
Many long years ago I was a lamb
That nestled by Jesus when he was a baby.

I helped keep him warm, and that is no maybe.
But time doesn't stop and a sheep's what I am.

Now, normally sheep do not live long as me,
However, I'm limping, and obviously
That means though in all other ways I am nice
I'm not perfect enough for a pure sacrifice
At the temple. That suits me just fine, to be sure.
There's no doctor for sheep, so I won't get a cure.

When Jesus was near me, I kept him quite warm.
The Lord of all living should know no alarm.
He lay by my side and I kept very still
So the infant would keep very warm and not ill.

Now say what you will, but it's true. Since that day
My fleece has been perfect. Whatever you say,
You have to admit that my coat's good for shearing
And year after year at each spring's appearing
My fleece, and I say this quite humbly, is best
And is worth more at market than all of the rest.

Now, thirty years later upon a green hill
I saw Jesus again, as I hope you all will.
He was speaking to many who looked on with hope,
The sad sort of people who barely can cope
With poverty, misery, things that would try ya,
All praying that Jesus would be the Messiah.

And while he was talking, he beckoned me over
Just like an old friend that we might rediscover.
He patted my head, the Good Shepherd, and told
The people how long ago prophets of old
Had pointed to one who the sheep would remember
And follow no matter, in March or December.

We sheep know a shepherd from one who's a thief.
And he who would lead us to blessed relief.
By pastures of green or waters so still
Where sheep may eat plenty and drink up their fill
Is one that we honor, or nobody either.
Just trust me. This one's from the Heavenly Father.
Yes, he's the Good Shepherd. My promise I keep.
And who would know shepherds much better than sheep!

That's the last that I saw him; I wish that I knew
What's happened to Jesus. Oh, what will we do?

Gabriel
I know of his birth. Tell me what happened next!
This lamb has been helpful, but I'm still perplexed.

Wonderful
And I'm just as puzzled. The carpenter's son
Grew up and built furniture in shade and sun.
I've found in my travels this table he hammered
And find in our talking that I'm quite enamored.
And wood should the good tell for wood understood.

Gabriel
I suppose wood would tell us if anyone could.

The Table
I am the table that Jesus constructed
On the day when he set aside all of his tools
To do what his Heavenly Father instructed
Distilling the law into two easy rules,
To love God and neighbors the sum of the law,
Which is clear to see as a very sharp saw!

He planed me and sanded and pounding he hammered.
It pained me. Unhanded, and surely ungrammared,
Against my own will for I can't speak a word.
I failed to warn him and here's what occurred.
A splinter of mine pricked his innocent finger.
His blood dripped upon me and there did not linger
But soaked into wood and it coated a nail,
And nothing will pry the blood loose, not a gale.

And that was the end. He was finished with me
When someone came by and said much company
Was coming, and quickly she needed a table
To serve up some food, just as soon as was able.

No money changed hands. As a gift to that friend
I set forth on a journey that still has no end.
This Nazareth friend loved this table so well
That she gave it away and the way that things fell
As a secondhand treasure in a caravan grand
Past sea that is salty and hot desert sand

I came to Jerusalem. It was my doom
To wait in a dusky and dim Upper Room.

When the Passover Meal was eaten one day
Then was Jesus among all the ones who could stay
To drink and break bread and share wonderful food.
Their feet he had washed, and his body and blood
He offered for all of humanity's sin.
I listened intently. His blood was within
My wood after all of these years, don't you think?
And when he was through, Jesus gave me a wink.

But that's all I know. With Passover through
They left singing psalms. And me? What could I do?

Gabriel
Our thanks go to you, Oh, most marvelous table
Who willingly told us two all you were able.

Wonderful
And waiting outside, while the twelve walked away,
This colt, quite content was still patient to stay,
In case he was needed. He said he would bide
For once he had given to Jesus a ride.

Gabriel
Then tell us, dear colt, while your memory's clear.
What happened down there while we waited up here.

The Colt
Higgledy Piggledy
Jesus once rode on me
Into Jerusalem.
All there could see

Savior and Lord was he
Ruling eternally
Over the lot of them
Fantastically.

Poggledoms, Hoggledoms
All that he's saying calms!
Honor him, Allelyu!
Then, without qualms

All the poor, needing alms
Cheered him while waving palms
Glory him, story him,
Gideon's balms.

Gabriel
Is anyone left who can tell us the story
Of whatever happened to Jesus of glory?

Wonderful
I found two more things in my travels on earth.
You listen to them and then judge of their worth.

The Cross
Rough hewn, grown tough, not my will
But destiny a bitter pill
Has set me cruelly on a hill.
Now all is still.

Only evil could death's engine
In their mind devise. Dissension
Against Rome provides the victims
Who — and this is reprehension —
Hang in pain by royal dictums
Nails tearing anguished tendon,
Until extinguished without mention.

I've no choice. Yes. I saw Jesus.
He is dead. This should not please us.
Others taunted. What was meant
Executing innocent
And instructing prophets? Please
Tell me what was meant by these?

Gabriel
These words have filled my soul with dread.
You cannot mean that he is dead.

Wonderful
I mean the same, but there is more.
There is some startling news in store.

The Stone
Archimedes said with a lever he'd move
The earth from its settled foundation.

I was quite happy to rest in this grove
Covering graves for the health of the nation.

Ashes to dust and the dust goes to ashes,
It's all the same, whether lips or eyelashes.
When life is over they come to the tomb.
All of humanity shares the same doom.

Say it's my job to preserve bad and best
Lying in state while they're taking their rest.

Some still assert when it's time for the end
All their constituent sinews will mend.
Bones that are dry will take on flesh and blood
And stand at attention. The judge, who is good,
Will weigh them and measure them, but that their price
Is paid by the Savior who never thought twice
And died for them willingly, there on the cross,
Intentionally suffering horror and loss.

It happened. And Joseph of Arimathea
Donated the space where I'm waiting to see ya.
I'm who guards sepulcher, slab, box, and niche,
Who harbors the poor and who gathers the rich.

I never lost one that they gave me to guard,
But sheltered the dead without any regard
To their merit or lack of it, and I'm here to say
That Jesus the Lord, he is risen today!
They brought him here broken up on a crude cross
His flesh had been nailed, his back the emboss
Of thirty-nine lashes he patiently bore
Impressed with a cruelty all should abhor,
And a thorny crown pressed all the way to the bone,
And naked they hung him to die all alone.
The wind howled. Rain fell. In the day it was dark.
The curtain was torn in the temple. The stark
Bitterness deadly now gave way to blessings.
The women had come after Sabbath with dressings
To pay last respects to the one they adore,
And I, who am given to guard death's own door,
Was rolled away, bowled away. Fold away cloths
Intended to wrap up a corpse. Let the moths
Devour the garments intended for death.
This Jesus is living. The Lord will draw breath

Eternally, first fruits of all who are sleeping.
The ancestors who in their limbo were keeping
A watch for their Savior they knew through the Bible
Was coming were rescued by he who they libel
In trial they trumped up. Triumphant is he
Who rules earth and heaven, both eternally.

I am the stone who was guarding the grave
Of the one who left heaven's throne, happy to save
Each one of you. Angels, rejoice; people, sing.

Wonderful
The new age has started. Let every bell ring.
Our Lord wasn't missing. His mission's completed.

Gabriel
And now upon heaven's throne he will be seated.
Each voice should be raised. Each memory treasured,
All songs should be written in meter unmeasured
To tell of his glory.

Wonderful
Let this lesson teach you
When next you leave heaven for rest or for slumber
Make sure that you leave me a way we can reach you,
Celestial addresses or some kind of number!

Tongues
Of Fire

A Choral Reading
For Pentecost

Kenneth Carlson

Tongues Of Fire

This reading was written for four voices.

Voice 1: Jesus had gathered a motley crew

Voice 2: Around him he gathered the lost and the lame

Voice 3: The least and the last

Voice 4: Around him he gathered uneducated fishermen

Voice 3: And educated tax collectors

Voice 1: Within this band of ragtag followers there were no priests

Voice 2: There were no Pharisees

Voice 4: There were no men of wealth

Voice 3: There were no men of influence

All: Jesus had gathered a motley crew

Voice 4: Yet the grace of God had blessed them

Voice 2: The grace of God had embraced them

Voice 1: The grace of God had found a way to use their words and hands

Voice 3: Words to express the new creation in Christ

Voice 4: Hands to express the open hospitality of love

Voice 2: Many came to see this Man of God

Voice 3: Many came to hear his words of power

All: Many came

Voice 1: Few remained

Voices 3/4: Sell your wealth

Voices 1/2: Give to the poor

Voice 4: But the rich man could not stay

All: He came

Voice 4: But he could not stay

All: Nicodemus came

Voice 1: He came beneath the shadows of night

Voice 2: He came to see for himself

Voice 3: He came to hear for himself

All: He came to see and hear

Voice 4: He heard a word of rebirth and promise

Voice 3: He saw a man of truth and grace

All: Nicodemus remained

Voice 1: But many like him fell by the way

Voice 2: Healthy seed that would never germinate

Voice 3: Healthy seed that would never put down strong roots

Voice 4: Healthy seed that would never bear good fruit

All: Jesus had gathered together a very motley crew

Voice 3: They were called drunkards and sinners

Voice 2: Vagrants and outcasts

Voice 4: They were dismissed as wayward children

Voice 1: They were seen as rebellious troublemakers

Voices 2/3: They used the Sabbath to offer ministry

Voices 1/4: While others let the Sabbath use them for nothing

Voice 1: They heard the voice of despair and offered hope

Voice 3: They heard the voice of pain and offered healing

Voice 2: They heard the voice of betrayal and offered trust

Voice 4: They heard the voice of need and offered bread

Voice 1: This was a word that could not be stopped

Voice 2: This was a word that would move beyond the words of the baptist

Voice 3: This was a word that would transcend water with fire

All: This was a word that would encircle the world

Voice 4: But for now it moved at the speed of walking feet

Voice 1: It moved from city to city

Voice 3: It moved from town to town

Voice 2: It moved with the deliberate pace of one who knew his mind

Voice 1: Of one who knew his purpose

Voice 4: Of one who knew God's mind and God's purpose

Voices 1/4: It moved from healing to healing

Voices 2/3: From sacred touch to prayerful blessing

Voice 1: It moved as a wave that could not be stopped

Voice 4: A wind that could not be contained

Voice 2: Yet all the while a lonely hill stood waiting to receive its guest

All: Calvary stood waiting

Voice 4: And it was only a matter of time

Voice 1: A blessed entrance with singing and shouting

All: Blessed is he who comes in the name of the Lord

Voice 2: A blessed meal with prayer and foot washing

All: This is my body

Voice 3: Take and eat

All: This is my blood

Voice 1: Take and drink

All: Be forgiven

Voice 4: Embrace the abundant life

Voice 2: Embrace the love I have for you

Voice 1: Do for each other what I have done for you

Voice 3: Do for everyone what God has done for you

Voice 4: A promise was made in that small room that night

Voice 2: A promise was made that would bear fruit likes tongues of fire

Voice 1: It was a promise that came with a price

Voice 3: It was a price that no one wanted to pay

Voice 4: Jesus said he would be betrayed that night

Voice 3: He would be taken away from them

All: Separated and apart

Voices 1/2: But they should not worry

Voices 3/4: They should not be anxious

All: Because God would send another

Voice 2: A Spirit of truth

Voice 1: A Spirit of grace

Voice 3: A Spirit of power

Voice 4: A Spirit of fire beyond water

Voices 1/3: God would not leave them in their fear and sorrow

Voices 2/4: Jesus would not leave them without his blessing

Voice 1: My peace I give you

Voice 2: My peace I leave you

Voice 3: Let not your hearts be troubled

Voice 4: Neither let them be afraid

All: But Jesus had gathered a motley crew

Voices 1/4: In spite of his words

Voices 2/3: In spite of his promise

All: They fled

Voice 1: One denied him

Voice 2: One betrayed him

Voices 3/4: All deserted him

Voice 4: But God would not deny him

Voice 3: God would not betray him

Voices 1/2: God would not desert him

All: It was just a matter of time

Voice 4: Within hours their Jesus was arrested and tried

Voices 2/3: Beaten and bruised

Voice 1: Within a day he was mocked and spat upon

Voices 2/3: Crucified and buried

Voice 4: Within two days they had forgotten everything he said

Voice 2: Within two days grief had numbed their hearts

Voice 3: Within two days his death had destroyed their hopes

Voices 1/4: But on the third day their sorrow turned to joy

Voices 2/3: Their grieving turned to celebration

All: He was not dead — he was alive

Voice 1: And for forty days he dwelt among them

Voice 3: Eating and drinking

Voice 2: Offering and remembering

Voice 4: He broke bread and they remembered

Voice 2: He shared the cup and they remembered

Voice 1: He talked of the Spirit and they remembered

All: And in all these years things have not changed

Voices 1/2: In the breaking of the bread we remember

Voices 3/4: In the sharing of the cup we remember

Voice 3: Wherever two or more are gathered in his name we will remember

Voice 4: This is *my body* broken for you and for all

All: So you may have life

Voice 1: This is *my blood* shed for you and for all

All: For the forgiveness of sin

Voice 2: I will not leave you alone

Voice 3: God will not leave you alone

Voice 4: Someone will come after me and remind you of all I said and taught

All: And so they waited — it was only a matter of time

Voice 2: They selected Matthias to replace Judas among the twelve

All: And they waited

Voice 4: They went about their daily business

All: And they waited

Voice 1: They held dear the promise of their Lord

Voice 2: They held dear the Light of the World

Voice 3: They held dear the Bread of Life and the Good Shepherd

Voice 4: They held dear this precious hope

All: And they waited

Voice 3: They waited as one who expects a guest to arrive at the door

Voice 4: They waited as one who expects gifts beneath a tree

Voice 1: They waited for the promise of their Lord to be fulfilled

Voice 2: They went about their business

All: And they waited

Voice 4: It came as a wind that could not be contained

Voice 2: It came as a sound that could not be stopped

Voices 1/3: It came as fire and smoke and rested upon their heads

Voice 4: Many saw it and embraced this wind as the promise of new life

Voice 2: They hugged the sound as if their lives depended upon it

Voices 1/3: Others denied the moment

Voice 4: Turned their heads in disgust at such drunken behavior

Voice 2: But Peter would not let them leave

Voice 1: Peter would not let them diminish the moment

Voice 3: Nor would he let them denigrate the memory

Voice 2: Peter would preach and say: Thus says the Lord

Voice 1: I will pour out my Spirit on all people

Voice 3: I will show wonders in the heavens above

Voice 2: Young men will see visions

Voice 4: Old men will dream dreams

All: Both men and women will receive my Spirit

Voice 1: Peter would tell the story of Jesus

Voice 2: He who lived among you, and was crucified, still lives

Voice 3: He who healed your sick and gave life to those who sat in darkness lives forever

All: God has raised him from the dead

Voice 4: God has freed him from the darkness of death

Voice 2: God has made death a servant of his grace

Voice 3: And for this gift our lives shall ever be changed

Voices 1/3: We will not be shaken

Voices 2/4: We will not be moved

Voice 1: John came with water to cleanse our sins

Voice 4: Jesus comes with fire to burn away our shame

Voice 3: We may be a motley crew but we are not drunk

All: The Spirit of the Lord is upon us

Voice 1: And every ear shall hear these words of truth regardless of their nation and their tongue

Voice 4: Every ear shall hear that Jesus lives

Voice 2: Every heart shall be lifted up

Voice 3: And every voice declare

All: Alleluia and hosanna

Voice 4: Blessed is he who comes in the name of the Lord

Voice 3: Blessed is he who died and lives forever

Voice 2: Blessed is the resurrection and the life

Voice 1: For we shall all die yet shall we live

Voice 3: Recognize the truth of what we say

Voice 1: Recognize the power of our words

Voice 2: Recognize the grace already burning within your hearts

Voice 4: Recognize Jesus as Lord of all

All: And let the Holy Spirit come upon you

Voice 1: Let it burn away your shame

Voice 2: Let it cleanse you from your sin

Voice 3: Let it possess your life with eternal hope and everlasting light

All: Water was honored and 3,000 were baptized

Voice 4: Three thousand who heard a word they had not really heard before

Voice 2: Three thousand who thought their lives were complete and fulfilled

Voice 3: Three thousand who never expected to be touched by anything, much less fire

Voice 4: Three thousand joined the ranks of the transformed

Voice 2: Three thousand placed their trust in the grace of God

Voice 1: Three thousand experienced something so new they could not wait to tell others

All: And neither can we

Voice 1: The Spirit of God exists to this day

Voice 2: The Pentecost of yesterday is the transformed witness of today

Voices 3/4: The fruit of the Spirit expresses our gratitude

Voices 1/2: The presence of the Spirit expresses our faith

Voice 1: The peace that Jesus gave his disciples on that hallowed night 2,000 years ago

Voice 4: Is still the peace we receive through faith today

All: As the Spirit moves

Voice 3: So does the power of our witness

Voice 1: May God continue to bless us and keep us

Voice 2: May God continue to give us the light of his Son and our Savior, Jesus Christ

Voice 3: May God continue to grant us peace for the day

Voice 4: And hope for all that is yet to come

Voices 1/2: May God continue to pour upon us the blessings of his Spirit

Voices 3/4: As we recall the words of faith

Voice 2: Let not your hearts be troubled

Voice 1: Neither let them be afraid

Voices 1/2: God has touched us with his fire

All: And nothing will ever be the same again

Contributors

Kenneth Carlson is an ordained United Methodist elder who is currently the pastor of Rifle United Methodist-Presbyterian Church in Rifle, Colorado. He is a former radio disc jockey, as well as a song and story writer whose credits include two tapes of recorded music. Carlson is a graduate of Morningside College and Iliff School of Theology.

David H. Covington is an associate professor of English at North Carolina State University, specializing in professional writing and Victorian literature. An active member of the Kirk of Kildare (Presbyterian) in Cary, North Carolina, he is a graduate of the University of Florida (B.A.) and Vanderbilt University (M.A., Ph.D.).

John O. Eby has been an ordained pastor for four decades, serving several Baptist congregations in California. He is currently the pastor of First Baptist Church in Porterville, California. A graduate of the University of LaVerne and American Baptist Seminary of the West, Eby is the author of more than thirty skits and plays.

Kathy Martz is a former schoolteacher who combines a strong religious affiliation with professional training in psychology and education to produce creative, inspirational writings for a Christian audience. She is an active member of Christ Lutheran Church in Oakwood, Georgia, and is a graduate of Alma College and Oakland University.

Will Rabert is a retired United Church of Christ pastor who served congregations in Pennsylvania for nearly forty years. He is the co-author of the children's play *The Littlest Christmas Tree* (CSS).

Frank Ramirez is the pastor of Everett Church of the Brethren in Everett, Pennsylvania. A graduate of LaVerne College and Bethany Theological Seminary, Ramirez is the author of numerous books, articles, and short stories. His CSS titles include *Coming Home*, *He Took A Towel*, *The Christmas Star*, *A Call To Worship*, and *Lectionary Worship Aids*.

Carol Secord is director of senior adult ministry at Rivermont Presbyterian Church in Chattanooga, Tennessee. A graduate of Auburn University, Secord has had three of her plays published by national distributors.